Like Barbarians in India

Like Barbarians in India

Jean-Claude Perrier

Translated from the original French
Comme des barbares en Inde
by

Sriparna Chatterjee

NIYOGI
BOOKS

The Work is published with the support of the Publication Assistance Programmes of the Institut français

First English edition published by Niyogi Books, 2022

Published by
NIYOGI BOOKS
Block D, Building No. 77
Okhla Industrial Area, Phase-I
New Delhi-110 020, INDIA
Tel: 91-11-26816301, 26818960
Email: niyogibooks@gmail.com
Website: www.niyogibooksindia.com

Editor: K.E. Priyamvada
Design: Shashi Bhushan Prasad
Cover design: Akankshya Padhi

Front cover image: Detail from *The Kiss*, by Jean-Baptiste Jules Trayer, 1858
Rear cover image: Detail from *The Empress Josephine*,
by Pierre-Paul Prud'hon, c.1805

ISBN: 978-93-91125-16-5
Publication: 2022

Printed at Niyogi Offset Pvt. Ltd., New Delhi, India

Jean-Claude Perrier

Like Barbarians in India

— Loti, Michaux, Malraux, Gide —

Essay

In memory of Catherine Gide (1923–2013)
who never went to India, but loved Nepal.

Contents

Prologue

'It's your karma', my Hindu friends tell me. Hardly anything in this realm surprises them. What if, in a previous life, I had been born a Brahmin, performing religious rituals all day long, my bare chest girded with the sacred white cotton thread, surrounded by garlands of multicoloured flowers, incense and ghee, the clarified butter with which one anoints idols? Or if I had been a 'sadhu', renouncing all the vanities of this world to devote myself to the sole divinity? Or even, a 'dalit', an untouchable? And who knows if, in one of my future births, I will not be that sacred elephant, blessing the crowds with his trunk for a few rupees, outside the small Ganesh Temple in Pondicherry? One would like to believe in reincarnation.

Even now, and it has been almost 35 years since my first maiden trip, not a day goes by when I don't think of India, that I don't long to return. Even though the experience is not always easy, and the evolution of the country, even in its most remote corners, is annoying. With every visit, I find more concrete, more noise, and more pollution. In the summer of 2013—I hadn't been back since the first Bonjour India festival in 2009—I wanted to do a test. I settled in for a month, alone, in the heart of a Tamil village in the union territory of Pondicherry, just half an hour from the nearest metropolis, just to see if the charm still worked on me; if, after four years of being away, I would still love India. There was this terrifying, dizzying risk of not loving it anymore. I was, as on the very first day, overwhelmed, dazzled, unsettled, annoyed, stunned...but throbbing with life. Life here is more intense, more elemental. Each time I set foot on the soil of Bharat, I feel a considerable energy rushing through me, as if by some rejuvenating transfusion. And then, of course, there are the perfumes, the colours, these people of 'bronze chests and beautiful black velvet eyes', in the words of Loti, whose splendour never ceases to strike the Westerner with wonder. This profusion. India is the country of excesses, of too much.

Until now, I have hardly dared to write about India, except for the travel diaries of an incredible journey through our former trading posts.[1] This is mostly out of a fear of feeling 'inadequate'; as Gide had felt in the presence of the masterpieces at the Hermitage Museum when he went to Leningrad in 1936 (before it had been renamed Saint Petersburg). Then again, I had done a lot of work, on contemporary Indian literature, and also on the relationship with India of some of my favourite French writers, whom I call my 'gurus': Loti, Malraux, Gide. To this list, since I have been offered an opportunity to return to this Indophilia that brings us together, I now add Michaux. India, discovered by him in 1931, occupies the first half of his book *A Barbarian in Asia*. An India, about which he has waxed lyrical with this line: 'India sings, do not forget that, India sings.'

It is again Michaux, who while re-writing the preface to his book in 1967, affirmed that, 'Here, barbarian we were, barbarian we must remain'. Applied to Loti and Malraux, who have travelled in India, and to Gide, who never actually went to India,

1 In Jean-Claude Perrier's *Dans les Comptoirs de l'Inde–Carnets de Voyage*, new edition (Imperiali Tartaro, 2013).

but experienced it in his own way, this epithet is in no way pejorative. It defines a relationship, the only one that, paradoxically, allows a Westerner to see clearly the reality of the country: fascinated, bewitched certainly, but 'barbaric'. To remain true to oneself is the only way to discover, to learn, to admire, and to love India passionately, while preserving one's own identity, one's own methods of analysis. As opposed to all these young people who, since the 1960s, usually with good intentions, have come to India to lose themselves under the pretext of finding themselves (again)! Amongst more than a billion Indians, what could be easier? And more illusory, too. One is born an Indian, one does not become one, or else, only with extreme difficulty. Just as Hinduism, the religion of the vast majority, does not proselytise nor encourage conversions.

This book is thus an invitation to find in Mother India—in the land, its inhabitants, its culture, its writers—some illustrious guides, whose relationship with this 'country of ancient civilization', according to Malraux's beautiful formula, we will seek to explore. And even if each of them has, all considered, written relatively little about India.

As a literary archaeologist of some miraculous finds—concerning Gide, for example—I will blend in my own Indian pages, fruits of my travels, my experiences, encounters and impressions reconstructed retrospectively. I will try to fill in the gaps each time. With each visit, even to the places where I have already been, I learn. A 'Barbarian' no doubt, but in love. And, so impatient to go back again.

I

Pierre Loti in India (Without the English)

Strangely enough, considering his spiritual expectations, his enthusiasm, and the excellent quality of the book that his travels had inspired in him—*L'Inde (sans les Anglais)*, one of his masterpieces—India transpired quite late in the travels of Pierre Loti. He made only one long journey there from the 20th of December 1899 to 25th March 1900—it seems that, for this voyage, we can rely on the chronology that he provides us with, in spite of certain grey areas and large approximations which were common occurrences in his writings. Despite his apparent meticulousness, our man is not a master of precision.

In 1899, Julien Viaud of Rochefort was 49 years old. He had undertaken his first voyage in 1868, on the *Bougainville*, as a midshipman. He had just been promoted to the rank of Captain of the frigate, after having been reinstated in the navy, but had been placed on shore-leave, unpaid and without an assignment, at the discretion of the Minister of Foreign Affairs (who was his friend, the radical Théophile Delcassé), until 25 July 1900. It would be these 'holidays' that he would put to good use to travel extensively, in complete freedom—in a private capacity but entrusted with a few missions which were more or less official, even secret—and to forget his humiliation of 1898. Then a lieutenant, Julien Viaud had, like 27 other officers, been placed under mandatory retirement by his minister, under the pretext of 'rejuvenating the cadres'! Bureaucratic stupidity is a common occurrence in all eras. The affair sparked many protests, and finally ended in a victory for the 'retirees'. As of 2 August 1900, the frigate captain would resume active service, cruising towards China at the height of the Boxer Rebellion. But that is another of his stories.

As for his alter ego, the writer Pierre Loti, he was officially born on 2 October 1880 in an article in *Le Monde Illustré*. Almost all of his work appeared in the press and in magazines before being collected, reviewed and edited by him, then by his son Samuel, in numerous volumes, published mostly by Calmann-Lévy. Previously, his first novels, *Aziyadé* and *Le Mariage de Loti* (The Marriage of Loti) had been published by Calmann-Lévy, anonymously, in the beginning of 1879 and in the spring of 1880 respectively. The first was a flop. The second, however, labelled 'by the author of *Aziyadé*', found immediate and 'resounding' success. After which, Viaud would sign all his articles and works with his pseudonym, brought back from his enchanting journey to Tahiti in 1872. 'Loti' was a distortion of 'roti' (with an r rolled to something akin to our l), the word for rose or laurel (oleander) in Tahitian. His friend, the Queen Pomaré, who would have bestowed on him this nickname, undoubtedly, possessed a blessed gift of clairvoyance, because from 1881 onwards, with *Roman d'un spahi,* his first title signed Pierre Loti, the writer was to gather many laurels. Prolific (one to two novels or travelogues per year), famous, he was even elected to the French Academy. In 1891, in the sixth round, he was pitted against, among others, Émile Zola (who got zero votes), which some imbeciles would reproach him for, for a long time.

The youngest of the Quai de Conti,[2] however, did not care, and it was indeed his status as an academician that would lead him to India in 1899.

Earlier, Loti had made a first contact, though briefly, with the subcontinent, under unusual circumstances. Right in the beginning of 1886 (and not in 1884, as the editors estimate, he would have been incorrect by two years, though one is not sure why), when he published an account of his stay *Propos d'exil*—in 1887—Julien Viaud's ship, *La Corrèze*, on its way back from Tonkin, made a three-day stop-over off the Indian coast, opposite Mahé, in the state of Kerala.

Mahé was—and it still is, a very special India. From 1721 to 1954—the year of the restitution of jurisdiction by France to India of its four remaining settlements, (Chandernagor in Bengal having taken the lead earlier by referendum in 1949) the small tropical town, Mahé, languishing on the banks of the river whose name it bears, was one of the trading posts of the Royal India Company, created by Colbert, in the midst of a paradise of spices: home of the precious pepper, in

2 **Editor's note:** The Institut de France is located at 23 Quai de Conti and it includes the Académie Française, which elected Pierre Loti (1850–1923) a member in 1891. This meant that at age 41 he was one of the youngest members, hence 'the youngest of the Quai de Conti'.

particular, which the British, established, not far away, in Tellicherry, were fighting over.

The officer Julien Viaud would remain at sea, on his boat, but the author Pierre Loti would go ashore every day, to wander, to roam as he wished and as the opportunities arose. He was thus invited to a wedding where he witnessed some rather exotic (and 'erotic') dances, which, even to the eyes of a seasoned traveller like him, reminded him a little of the beloved Polynesia of his youth. Throughout his life, Loti experienced, and frequently expressed, a nostalgia for lost paradises, of a happy childhood which was forever gone, this would sustain the *taedium vitae* of his restless soul, haunted by the idea of death and in search of a faith that could ward it off—knowing that the Christianity in which he had been raised had disappointed him: 'I have tried to remain Christian but I failed', he confided on several occasions.

In Mahé, Loti would go along the river, take a tour of the governor's residence (which still exists, with its park of teak, mango, jackfruit and coconut trees and precious pepper vines), visit the cathedral dedicated to Saint Teresa of Avila (which still remains as white and dapper), and would be welcomed into the home of the natives whose children recited for him 'The Wolf and the Lamb', by the good M. de La Fontaine. Soon after, at the invitation of two young guides, orphans to whose charm he shows himself to be susceptible, he would venture into the middle of the jungle to see a small 'pagoda', a term used at that time, which was in fact, a temple to Ganesh, 'a very small monster (...), having vaguely the head of an elephant on the body of a man', the first of a series of Hindu gods and temples with which he would later become familiar.

Nature is lush, generous and abundantly described by the writer, who recalls the forest of his native Saintonge. It is obvious that Loti was captivated by this 'India of palms', as he calls it, this ancient Hindu Dravidian land, pagan and sensual, which he would hold in contrast with northern India, that of the Muslim Mughals, the 'starving India'. With its real sweetness of life, even if one does not disregard its problems. Our friend is especially enamoured with the locals, the dark beauty of the South Indians: 'The people we meet are all beautiful, calm, noble, with big velvet eyes—those Indian eyes with a mysterious black charm.'

At the end, he abandons himself to his graceful and mischievous guides, who invite him to follow a noisy and colourful procession. 'Here, it is India; it is in India that I am', he insists, as if struggling to convince himself of the exhilarating reality that he is experiencing, 'in the India of bronze chests and beautiful black velvet eyes—in the hot, exuberant, splendid India!'

This first meeting is, literally, love at first sight. 'Well, then yes, I will follow them (his guides, and the "bronze Indians" in general), I will go to see...,' concludes Loti. He certainly had a strong intuition that he would return to India. To see, and that would be 13 years later.

***

At the end of 1899, while Captain Julien Viaud was still on unpaid leave, the writer Pierre Loti accepted a very pleasant assignment. On behalf of the Académie Française, he was commissioned to go and present to His Highness, the Maharaja of Travancore, in person and at his palace in Trivandrum, the Cross of the *Chevalier dans l'Ordre des Palmes Académiques*. He would take the opportunity to travel around India, following a rather unrealistic itinerary that no modern tour operator would dream of proposing to his clients! Coming from Colombo, the capital of the island of Ceylon, he disembarks south of the Coromandel Coast, and makes his way to Trivandrum, where he scrupulously fulfils his task, then explores at leisure his 'India of palms', Kerala and Tamil Nadu. However, while staying in Pondicherry, instead of proceeding to nearby Madras (about 150 kilometres away), he heads due north, towards 'starving India', Rajasthan. Then he finally descends towards Madras, continues eastwards to Andhra Pradesh, heads back to Delhi and completes his grand tour, symbolically, in Benares. Was this really the end of his travels? That is what he would want us to believe in *India (without the English)*. For, in reality, he continued from Benares towards Calcutta, from where he travelled for a day to Rangoon, and back. What was the purpose, tourism or a 'geographical and economic mission' for his government? Among the grey areas that remain with Loti, who frequently 'disappeared' in this way, it would be necessary to study these famous missions closely. Perhaps they were those of a secret agent, a spy? After Calcutta, he headed for Bombay, from where he left India forever, bound for Persia, via Muscat. He arrived there in April 1900. Yet another 'mission' of which we know nothing.

As for the Lotian chronology, though seemingly meticulous, more often than not it turns out to be quite imaginary. At times it does not exist, at others, the episodes are not dated. Or, the writer is inaccurate; after verification by the specialists, who try to retrace his journeys step by step, the indicated dates prove to be implausible. Or else, certain sequences of the journey are not integrated into his account, written on the spur of the moment but then reworked and edited for publication, first as excerpts in the press and then as a volume. As far as India is concerned, Calcutta and Bombay are thus erased, and we can only regret that. Next to the apocalyptic pages that the slums of the Bengali metropolis—which was still the turbulent capital of the British Raj for 10 years—could have inspired in Loti, *The City of Joy* is but a trifle!

Let us follow Loti, who had left in search of the wisdom of the 'Sages of India', of this 'cradle of the soul and of prayer'. No longer for a 'frivolous stopover' of a few days (an allusion to his sojourn in

Mahé), but for a true initiation into the Hindu belief in the 'indefinite perpetuation of souls'. In other words, to put it simply, immortality through reincarnation.

Coming from Marseille, via the Suez Canal, he disembarked at Ceylon on 12 December 1899. He would stay there for a week, waiting for his Maharajah to be ready to receive him. 'And now it's India,' he exclaimed at the outset, which was both true and not so true. Certainly, the sister island has a close and mystical link with India, since one of the most famous episodes of the *Ramayana* took place there: the kidnapping of Rama's wife, the beautiful Sita, by the King of Lanka, the wicked Ravana, with his 10 heads and 20 arms. That is the Hindu side of the story. Yet Ceylon is also Buddhist, the religion of the majority Sinhalese. In Kandy, their ancient capital, which Loti visited, a temple even conserves a venerated relic, no less than a tooth of the Buddha.

After this initiation, during which he was as interested in Buddhism as he was in Hinduism, Loti crossed the Gulf of Mannar and disembarked at Tuticorin on 20th December. His entries up to 3 January 1900 are documented, but after that, there are no more points of reference. He heads immediately for Trivandrum, first in a bullock-cart, in which he travels lying down on his back—'a coffin', he notes. The jungle always reminds him of his native Saintonge. As for the Dravidian temples, with their towers on which are intertwined a multitude of statues, he admires them from the outside, since access to the inner sanctum is forbidden to non-Hindus. This is rare in India, where the Hindus are usually quite happy and proud to share their rituals and ceremonies with foreigners. On his way, this time by horse-drawn carriage, he finds interest in the Jews and the 500,000 Nestorian Christians who live in the region. He comes across wild tiger cats, deafening crows (one of the most characteristic sounds in the whole country), and wanders around a few temples whose proud and handsome priests, the 'brahmes' (now Brahmins), appeal to him greatly. On the 23rd, he finally reaches Trivandrum, the Forbidden City. The whole central area of the capital is occupied by a vast temple and a dark, labyrinthine palace, access to which is reserved to the Brahmins, the Maharajah, his family and the dignitaries of his court. Lodged outside the palace premises, the French guest was received the day after by His Highness, a well-read prince and a collector. The meeting was cordial, of course, but rather brief and a little disappointing. We would not know much about the exchanges between the monarch—clothed in the Indian fashion, and as Loti appreciated, not like an Englishman, in a frock coat—and the Academician, who, being fond of disguises, was presumably dressed in his official green embroidered habit, with his crocked hat under his arm and his sword at his side.

During the next four days, the visitor is treated with every courtesy: the Maharajah receives him again, sends an orchestra to where he is staying for a private concert, offers him a mini-parade of elephants, and invites him to meet his wife, the Maharani, as well as young women of the nobility adorned with their most lavish jewellery. Naturally, Loti attends all the religious ceremonies to which he is invited, and notices that, in this southern India, where he began his journey, there is a strong animist element that underlies Hinduism. Captivated, even though, after his departure from Trivandrum, he confides: 'I would not have guessed anything about Brahmanism', he shows a fine empathy and a profound openness of mind, which was not so common in his time, by writing: 'For there are no "false gods" and it is perhaps childish, the vanity of the wise who claim to possess the Truth, to know by what name it is called'. After which, on the 30th–31st, he sails by boat, where he can abandon himself to reverie and to meditation, as far as Quilon.

It was while he was in India that Loti crossed the turn of the 20th century, and he was delighted about that. He reached Cochin, where he was the guest of another maharajah ('in mourning'), in the house of the former Dutch governor. He enjoyed the attention, but felt a little 'trapped'. He was in a hurry to discover the real India, to be in direct contact with the people, as he had done everywhere, especially in Istanbul. Intensely curious about all religions, he visited the ghetto of the Jews in Matancheri, 'blues' (descendants of the Hebrews) or 'blacks' ('half-breeds converted in the past'); in Trichur, 'a very Brahminical city', a temple to Siva, a veritable fortress where he did not enter. After which, he took the express train to Madras, but allowed himself stopovers to visit the most sublime Dravidian temples of the region, dedicated to Vishnu or Siva: at Tanjore, Trichi, Srirangam (where he even spent the night), Madurai, where he attended a dance performance in Pali (ancient Sanskrit). The country, according to him, 'is one where worship is the most frenzied.' In a few hours, Loti sees everything, perceives the essential and recounts his story brilliantly.

From then on, the chronology fades away again. He savours 10 days in Pondicherry, 'our old, languid little colony', with 'that old charm of a homeland that nothing can replace'. He is the only tourist at his hotel. Then, instead of going to Madras, the English capital of the state, he bifurcates towards the white Hyderabad, the very Muslim capital of Andhra Pradesh, where he awaits, in vain, for the arrival of the Nizam. He visits the sights of Golconda, the phantom-city; Ellora, with its 'dreadful caves of death', and then proceeds by train to the Rajput country, Rajasthan.

The tone, here, changes. One now enters 'starving India'. Loti devotes strikingly written pages to the images of starving children, to rioters protesting for survival. In Udaipur, he indulges in social events, is received at the residence of the Maharajah, does a run of the temples, where he meets (as in Mahé earlier), two young Brahmins, two brothers, who serve as his guides, but in them he perceives 'a deep-rooted disdain for caste'. Well noted. He was also taken to meet 'rustic' fakirs who did not really impress him. In

Jaipur, he appreciates the city's 'pink cameo', but at the same time, he does not miss the hordes of beggars. He visits the ruins of Amber, and then moves on towards Gwalior: the Maharaja is absent; nevertheless, he is accorded a 'royal' reception at the palace, with its beloved elephants. He discovers Jain cave temples, before coming down, by train, towards the Gulf of Bengal, and its 'bronze nudes', that he much prefers to the 'swarthy pallor' of the Indians of the north.

Loti arrives in Madras, but he does not like it there at all. His discussions with two theosophists of the Institute founded by Annie Besant,[3] disappoint him. Their spiritualism, quite close to Buddhism, appears bland to him. As he moves towards Andhra Pradesh, he stops at the fortress-temple of Jagannath, where the priests deny him entry. As the train travels along the virgin beaches of the Bay of Bengal, he remembers the beaches of the Isle of Oleron(!) which, although he has spent his life travelling, arouse his 'invincible

3 Annie Besant (1847-1933), an English mystic who converted to theosophy, a doctrine that claims to integrate into Christianity a certain number of elements of Asian religions, including metempsychosis. She became president of the Theosophical Society and made many trips to India. Then she settled there, becoming, alongside Gandhi, an activist for Indian independence and the Congress Party, from which she would eventually separate. She died in Madras.

attachment to the native corner'. After Puri, he goes north again, still by train, to Delhi, the future capital of the British Indian Empire, a city that is calmer than the effervescent and dissenting Calcutta, where many intellectuals (such as Sri Aurobindo and Rabindranath Tagore) were early participants in the anti-colonialist struggle. He would simply be there as a tourist. On the way, he stops at Agra, 'the Muslim' emblem of the Mughal empire, its Red Fort and its Taj Mahal, 'the most impeccable mass of white marble in the world'. He seems to prefer his dark Tamil 'pagodas'.

Finally, we find Loti in Benares, the holiest city of Hinduism, a symbolic end of his mystical quest and the terminus of his literary journey. He spends most of his time on a boat on the Ganges, contemplating the cremations at the *ghats*. At the Maison des Sages, Annie Besant herself awaits him for a more intensive 'initiation' than the one in Madras. 'If I found nothing there, there would be nothing anywhere,' he confides. This 'esoteric Brahmanism' fascinates him. Does it bring him what he had come to look for? Loti returns tirelessly to the Ganges, meets the faithful indulging in their ritual ablutions, a dead yogi, a Pandit[4] who

4 From Sanskrit *pandita*, literate, the word designates a 'high-caste' Brahmin.

takes him for a walk in the countryside to see the bench on which the Buddha is said to have sat, various fakirs, monkeys, and a golden temple (where one does not enter). No raccoons. 'Oh, to die in Benares!' he exclaims, lyrically. 'To die on the banks of the Ganges, to have his corpse bathed there for the last time, to have his ashes scattered there!…' All he has to do is to conclude. A farewell ceremony in the form of a renunciation of the world, and humble thanks to the sages of Benares who, 'on the mysteries of life and death, hold the answers that best satisfy the ardent questioning of human reason'. In India, finally, the pilgrim found better than what he had come to seek and no longer received in the 'revealed religions': 'consolation'. Appeased, for once and for a moment, Loti the writer, faced with the Ineffable, then takes a vow of silence. Viaud, the traveller, continues his mad journey towards Calcutta, Rangoon, Bombay, Persia... and eventually, death.

L'Inde (sans les Anglais) appeared at the beginning of 1903, first as a serial in the *Revue des deux mondes*, then as a volume published by Calmann-Lévy, under its rather provocative title in the guise of a challenge : it is true that at no point of time is there any mention of the colonisers. And it is no coincidence that the writer's first contact with the country was in Mahé, and that he liked Pondicherry so much, both being French trading posts. Deeply patriotic, even chauvinistic, in the eyes of Loti, the English, like the Germans, were the hereditary enemy. All the more so for a sailor. And he never ceased, before the war of 1914–18, to stigmatise the 'anti-French' policy of 'the perfidious Great Britain', notably in the Middle-East and in Turkey. In addition to the title, it should be noted that *L'Inde (sans les Anglais)* is dedicated with fervour to Paul Kruger, President of the Republic of Transvaal, the future South Africa, and to his compatriots, repeatedly engaging in conflict with the British colonial power, notably during the Boer War, from 1899 to 1902, just before the publication of Loti's book. From 1893 until 1914, it was in this African country and in this tense context that a certain Mohandas Karamchand Gandhi, a young lawyer, undertook the non-violent struggle against the racial segregation that affected his fellow Indians. Gandhi, undoubtedly, was already dreaming, a formidable challenge to which he sacrificed his life, of an India without the British, like Loti. These two would surely have had a lot of things to talk about.

II

In Kerala, Where we Find Loti and Malraux

One hundred and seventeen years after Pierre Loti's brief visit, one may have the impression that Mahé has not changed. Nor have the charming old gentlemen Damodaran and Divakaran, who look like they have stepped out of a Tintin book. Slightly stooped, thin, bronze skinned, with immaculate hair and *veshti*—that South Indian cotton nether garment that is worn long or pulled up between the legs if you need to run or if it rains—black umbrella under the arm—it's the monsoon—they have come to solemnly welcome me at the airport of Kozhikode, once a Portuguese trading post where Vasco da Gama had landed, and formerly Calicut, where our calico came from. Today it is a big city of more than a million inhabitants on the Malabar coast, 62 kilometres to the north of Mahé, that is to say, at least two hours' drive on the crazy and pot-holed Highway 17, where—as in the rest of India—myriads of buses, coaches, trucks, cars, rickshaws and motorcycles rush by, in a frenzy of blaring horns, smoke and flashing headlights, while carts, bicycles, (sacred) cows and pedestrians try to make their way without risking their own lives. Priceless, even in the land of reincarnation. The whole office of the Alliance Française de Mahé has turned up in honour of the French guest, in a doddery old Ambassador where six of us, including the driver, are crammed in together.

The same ones, perhaps, served as guides to the naval officer Julien Viaud, alias Pierre Loti, through this small but distinctive piece of South India where he had ventured, and which he was to baptize so appealingly 'India of the palms,' as opposed to the north 'starving India', whose harsh reality he would discover, 13 years later. Kerala, in Malayalam, the language of the state, means 'Land of the Coconut Tree'. In Mahé, in 2003, children are still reciting 'The Wolf and the Lamb', and the portrait of M. de La Fontaine, next to those of his colleagues Rousseau, Voltaire and Hugo, still adorn the yellowish walls of the classroom of the venerable and modest Alliance

Française, with just a few dozen students, situated in the heart of the city. Fragile, but still valiant, almost half a century after France returned our former trading post to the young Indian Republic. Quite a significant symbol.

As a writer 'in residence' working on a book on the trading posts of India, it is from Mahé that I started my journey, which would end in Chandernagor, in West Bengal. This is simply a matter of geographical logic. The same journey would have been possible in the other direction. It didn't really matter. My idea was to make an inventory of all the traces of the French presence in these five former Indian territories: architectural, linguistic, cultural and human. Human, particularly. To meet witnesses who had lived through the colonial era, the liberation of the country and then the modern period. A rare privilege. And then, as the Africans say, an elder is like a library.

In Mahé, among the 'monuments' of the French presence, the old governor's palace, the cathedral, some colonial houses and bistros still exist. There was also a Mr and Mrs Sishupal. Both were freedom fighters, heroes of their country's struggle for independence, both Francophones and Francophiles.

Both delightful and charming. He, more expansive, begins to tell me, miming the most important scenes, about those decisive days in the summer of 1954 when, after a few forceful demonstrations, the Mahesians voted autonomously for the integration of their city with Mother India. With the French soldiers still on duty, taking refuge on a ship cruising off the coast—just like the ship, *La Corrèze*, with Loti on board in 1886—there was no confrontation. Mr Sishupal, the governor's accountant, had made it a point of honour that, despite the 'events', there was not a rupee missing from the safe. In the background, Mrs Sishupal, Karthy by name, looks on admiringly and lovingly at her husband as she did in the early days of their lives, even though she has had to endure the story of his exploits countless times. Sometimes he takes her hand, as if to solicit her approval, the corroboration of her memories. But he has a good memory, and concludes with panache: 'Everything we have accomplished here is thanks to France, which taught us about Revolution. Liberty, Equality, Fraternity.' Unstoppable.

Karthy, then a professor of French, had even served for a long time as the head of the French department at the University of Hyderabad,[5] in the capital—for the time being—of Andhra Pradesh, well to the east of Kerala, the state that includes the territory of another of our former trading posts, Yanaon (now Yanam). In 1973, as a young student, she had the opportunity to spend a year in France to complete her doctoral thesis, which she defended a year later at the University of Paris III-Sorbonne Nouvelle. Her thesis, unpublished at the time in her home country was titled 'Asia in the work of André Malraux'. Malraux, although already quite advanced in age and quite ill—he died in November 1976—lived in Verrières-le-Buisson, at the home of his dear friend Louise de Vilmorin (who

5 In the summer of 2013, the Indian government led by the Congress Party, the old party of Gandhi and Nehru, seems to have accepted the demand of an active minority of Telugu nationalists, the inhabitants of Andhra Pradesh, to split the current state into two separate states, one around the rich and high-tech capital, Hyderabad, christened Telangana, and the other retaining the rest of the territory, which is more agricultural and traditional, and therefore less favoured. In India too, the rich refuse to pay for the poor! I don't know where this unequal, absurd and ruinous 'reform' stands: the Indian administrative 'mammoth' being already oversized, doubling it seems to go against all current economic trends. Moreover, as I write these lines, the Congress Party is expected to lose in the April-May legislative elections to the BJP, the Hindu nationalist party. So will Telangana become India's 26th state, or will the project remain in the hands of a few demagogic politicians?
Editor's note: Telangana was declared a separate state from Andhra Pradesh on 2 June 2014, with Hyderabad as its capital.

died in 1969). He had retired and was receiving only very few visitors. He worked relentlessly to complete the last part of his work, and to reorganize it into the series he loved. Nevertheless, on the advice of her teacher, Karthy Sishupal requested an appointment with the great man, explaining who she was and what she was working on. And she was received. It was because she was Indian, obviously, and because Malraux maintained an exceptional, privileged and deep bond with India all his life. No doubt, he wanted to talk about India, as he was preparing to make his last private trip there in November: Delhi, Bombay...

Nevertheless, the young Indian woman spent an enchanting hour listening to the writer, returning to his favourite themes relating to the subcontinent and the major role he saw it playing in the history and geopolitical balance of the 21st century. Once again, he was right. Back home, Karthy deciphered the notes she had taken, organised them into an interview which she published, in English, in a modest academic journal. This text, which was offered to me spontaneously, has remained completely unpublished in French. She also gave me a letter that André Malraux had sent her after reading her 'edited' interview. Retranslated, I included it in the volume '*André Malraux et la tentation de l'Inde*' (André Malraux and the Temptation of India). Visiting my first French trading post, stumbling upon an important unpublished work by Malraux was a miracle, as I would experience several more in India, an infinite field of excavation for the literary archaeologist, the historian or the simply curious. Mrs Sishupal had kept in touch with the writer, who had sent her a copy of *Antimémoires*—his most 'Indian' book—and an autographed photo, treasures piously preserved by her, but all speckled with tropical mould. All of this must have disappeared today, but I had the privilege of seeing them. For my part, I had Gallimard, the publisher of Malraux, send a copy (published in 2004) to the Sishupals, imagining Karthy's surprise and delight, to see a photo of her featuring in it! Did they even receive it? I have not since returned to Mahé, a sort of end of the world, and I fear that the Sishupals, already very old, are no longer there.

***

Six years later, however, in Trivandrum, Ganesh did not favour me as much. Or, to be more precise, there was a breach in relations. That year, in 2009, I had been appointed the 'curator' for the literary part of the first Franco-Indian festival 'Bonjour India', by Culturesfrance, the cultural agency of our Ministry of Foreign Affairs, which would later become the French Institute. My role was to conceptualise a certain number of events, and send writers to different cities of the sub-continent (Delhi, Calcutta, Bangalore and Trivandrum), two or three to each place, to explain their work and thus promote French literature to a public that was generally young, cultured and French-speaking, those from the Universities and from the Alliances Françaises, which, in India, act as cultural centres. In addition to meetings with the authorities in Paris and Delhi, I wanted to visit the cities to see for myself whether the information had been disseminated, how things were being organised, how the reception was being prepared and whether everything was going well. And, among the cities I visited, I had chosen the distant Trivandrum, capital of Kerala, in the very south of the Indian peninsula, where Pascal Bruckner and Catherine Cusset were to go—as well as a young comic book author, invited by the Book Office. Of the four, it was the only city I didn't know, and whose modern name alone, in Malayalam, is enough to make you dream: Thiruvananthapuram. In the time of Loti, who landed there in late 1899, southern Kerala was called Travancore, and was the domain of a Maharaja.

What particularly struck me, in the pages of *India (without the English)*, which Loti devoted to this state, was his description of the temple and the royal palace of Trivandrum, a vast complex located in the heart of the city and forming a kind of forbidden city: reserved for the happy few Brahmins, prohibited to the *vulgum pecus*. Loti had been received several times at the palace, by the Maharajah and even the Maharani, but he had resided outside, in the newer sections of the city. As for the temple, it appears that at that time non-Hindus were not allowed entry. I confess that I have forgotten whether I ever went there. However, I did visit the main palace, which is now a museum—what remains of the once reigning family now reside in a more modest and discreet palace. It is a very dark labyrinth, suffocating, quite empty and ghostly, with its endless rows of unfurnished rooms, except for a few ugly armchairs, tired chests and large, completely pitted Venetian mirrors that could be mistaken for one-way mirrors. Here, one dares not speak loudly, or even breathe; it is as if the guardians of the past, hidden behind the mirrors, were spying on us. The hypersensitive Loti, so impressionable, would have had nightmares! And I confess my relief when my long wanderings came to an end. I am a bit claustrophobic.

During my brief stay, which was heavenly except for the myriad of particularly prolific and voracious mosquitoes—it seems everything went well for Bonjour India, and Catherine Cusset even romanticised her trip.[6] I had the privilege of meeting a young Malayali prince, one of the nephews of the present Rajah, who, like his fellow maharajahs, nawabs, or nizams, no longer has the power to rule ever since the feudal lords were officially abolished by Nehru, but retains a certain influence, and even remnants of splendour. Over a very friendly lunch, the exquisitely courteous Francophone prince explained to me that, had his own family been still ruling, he would never have wanted to take part in the race for power: for, in that family, it was customary for nephews to remove their uncles in order to succeed them, only to be killed in turn by younger and equally eager nephews!

6 Catherine Cusset, *Indigo* (Paris: Gallimard, 2013).

A peace-loving man, my host had instead chosen music. He had become a sitar virtuoso, performing on stages around the world. We talked at length about my old friend Ravi Shankar, the sitar God, who was still alive at the time;[7] and about many other things. He was very discreet about his family. He was clearly not happy about the subject. I tried to question him: where was the new palace located? And did he go there sometimes?

But my contrivances were too obvious. His Highness did not let himself be taken in. Unlike Loti, I was not received at the palace. But I blame myself for not having thought to ask if by chance, in the princely archives, assuming they had survived, there might not be some documents, some traces of the visit of the illustrious visitor, who had come with great pomp to honour the Maharajah. I would so much have liked to discover an unpublished photo of Loti in the grand costume of a French academician (at 40 degrees of tropical humidity), and of his host, dressed 'in the Indian style', (the writer specifies and appreciates that he was not dressed in the Western style) that is to say, in a silk *kurta* embellished with multi-coloured

7 Ravi Shankar passed away in December 2012.

embroidery and precious stones, his head crowned with an intricate turban adorned with an enormous diamond mounted with feathers.

Unforgivable oversight: I absolutely must return to Trivandrum one day, despite its mosquitoes. All the more so, as I missed out on another of its treasures. The city is famous, it appears, for its school of Kalaripayattu, a 3,000-year-old martial art, the forbear of all others, ritualized to the extreme and imbued with spirituality like everything else in India. It is similar to the Kathakali dance, which itself originated in Kerala. Nobody present at that time thought that this could interest me. The only consolation was: unless I am mistaken, Loti did not go there either. Too bad, he would have loved to see some of his beloved 'bronze chests' in motion, glistening with sweat. Instead, he was treated to a 'reception at the college of young girls of noble caste,' and processions of elephants, animals for which he felt a deep affection. So do I. In the teeming Hindu pantheon, Ganesh is my lucky God, the one who has watched over my travels for all these years. But when I went to Trivandrum, in October 2009, his mind was elsewhere; or he was angry with me for not praying to him enough during my pujas.

In India, whenever I can, which is often, I mingle with the crowd of worshippers who go to the temples to worship some God. I love this piety, which is at the same time, both demonstrative and personal, the *darshan*, its rites, the incense and the garlands of flowers with which the statues are adorned. Somewhat less so the ghee, the often rancid clarified butter with which the idols are anointed. I am Hindu as I am Catholic: aesthetically. Once when I was wandering around in Vailankanni, in southern Tamil Nadu, at a large Catholic shrine considered the 'Indian Lourdes', I saw my young driver, a die-hard Hindu, massaging the feet of a very Sulpician Christ and praying to him piously. And he, seeing my astonishment, said: 'You know, with the gods, you never know!' Like the ancient Romans, Hindus are fiercely pantheistic, not at all seeking to proselytize – it is almost impossible to convert to Hinduism – and rather willing to accept foreign deities, provided that other religious fanatics do not in any way impose on them that their God is the only one and the only one worthy of faith, and do not try to convert them. If that happens, they can be extremely violent. Not a day goes by in the country without a deadly clash between Muslim and Hindu fundamentalists, or even, in some regions, between Hindu and Catholic extremists, accused of spreading propaganda for their God. This is what the first missionaries, Franciscans or Jesuits, were accused of doing in Asia, and which got them into trouble. Loti too, who no longer found in the Christianity of his childhood something to quench his thirst for the absolute, felt close to Hinduism, fascinated by these superb 'Brahmins' who snubbed him—in the few temples where he was allowed entry! He had a perfect perception.

III

Michaux in India

In the summer of 1931, Henri Michaux decided to make his travel plan to Asia a reality. To travel on a cargo ship from Marseille to the Far East, as a regular passenger in economy class, or on the payroll as a steward, reliving his wild youth when he had travelled as a sailor to an unknown destination between 1919 and 1921.

This new adventure, shortly after the long journey to Ecuador in 1928, would have a profound impact on him, his life and on his work. He was deeply committed to it. Thus, in 1959, when he wrote, not without malice, his *Quelques renseignements sur cinquante-neuf années d'existence* (Some Information on Fifty-Nine Years of Existence), he included the phrase: '1930–1931, in Asia. Finally his journey', with an emphasis on the possessive and a chronological error to boot. This text would remain for a long time the only authorised biographical reference of a man who endeavoured all his life to remain in the shadows, to blur his tracks, and where he referred to himself in the third person.

Though it was indeed at the end of 1931 that Michaux embarked for Marseille, the exact date is unknown. But we do know, from one of his letters which was found later (he tore up, burned and threw away many books in his library), that he was in India, in Calcutta, at the beginning of January 1932. And that he was back in Paris before August 20th of the same year. Eight months, therefore, on a journey that was both long and far too short, given the scale of the programme. Little is known except through his correspondence and a major book, *Un barbare en Asie* (A Barbarian in Asia), published in one volume by Gallimard in 1933, in which India alone occupies more than half the pages: 'The Indians, the first people who, as a whole, seem to respond to the essential, who within the essential seek satisfaction, in fact a people that deserve to be distinguished from the others,' he commented almost 30 years later, in *Quelques renseignements*. In 1967, in his new Preface to the third version of his book, he explains: 'When I saw India, and when I saw China, for the first time, people on this earth seemed to me to deserve to be real.' The adjective is superb and perfectly accurate: all those who love India will say that, there, life is more intense, more essential and, yes, real.

But who is he, this Michaux of 1931, who is leaving again? A young writer in his 30s (he was born in Namur in 1899), brought up in a middle-class Belgian family where he always felt like a 'stranger', and who, instead of following a path which was well defined in advance, behaved like a 'failure': working at odd jobs, erratic and insecure. He nevertheless travelled a lot and published his first works in Belgian literary magazines (notably *Le Disque Vert*, written by his friend Franz Hellens) and in French. In Paris, where he would spend his life, he made his first friendships with elders whom he admired: Paulhan, Supervielle, meetings with Jouhandeau, Breton, Aragon....His first small book, was published at the beginning of the 1920s (*Les rêves et la jambe*—Dreams and the Leg), then came his entry into the NRF (La Nouvelle Revue Française) with *Qui je fus* (Who I Was) in 1927. This was followed by *Ecuador*. If he is not famous, if the sales of his books are rather modest—like those of most poets, even the greatest of the century—Michaux is not an unknown, he is read and appreciated by the happy few, hailed by a number of his peers. Though not by that old 'cockroach' Léautaud, who, in reference to *Voyage en Grande-Garabagne* (1935), spoke of 'complete nonsense' and 'ramblings without head or tail'! The writer also began to sketch: 'To decondition myself', he would later confess.

In the same way, still in the famous *Quelques renseignements* (Some Information) just before 1929, he writes: 'He travels against. To expel all signs of his homeland from himself'—Michaux, who hated to be reminded of his Belgian origins, would become a naturalized French citizen in 1955—'his ties of all kinds and those which have become part of him, in spite of himself, of Greek or Roman or Germanic culture'—a part of his mother's family is said to have come from the Rhineland—'or of Belgian habits. Journeys of expatriation.'

We note the contempt for Belgium, which is not entitled to the word 'culture' but to a more simple 'habits', we appreciate the beautiful formula, this trip against his personal history and origins. There will always be a rebel in Michaux. And this rejection of materialistic and decadent Western civilisation, this spiritual quest for elsewhere, this '*Drang nach Osten*' felt by the most sensitive, the most 'expatriated' of our writers: Loti, Segalen, Romain Rolland,[8] Daumal, Claudel, Malraux, among others...

Unlike his material baggage, which must have been quite modest, Michaux had not really 'prepared' his journey to Asia, and first to India, for several years, or at least not consciously, but had built up a kind of Indian 'cultural baggage' in the broader sense. Specialists, who are trying to reconstruct his overland itinerary step by step, have inventoried certain elements of it. Thus, as early as 1926, he advised his friend, the surrealist artist Claude Cahun, to go and see 'the Hindu village at the Jardin d'Acclimatation', with its elephants at work, which would become one of his totems. This passion was shared by Loti, then by Malraux. The elephant, an animal dedicated to Ganesh, one of the most important and popular gods of the Hindu pantheon,

8 Romain Rolland (1866–1944), winner of the Nobel Prize for Literature in 1916 for his pacifist stance, was very interested in Hinduism, author of, notably, *The Life of Vivekananda*, and of a biography of Mahatma Gandhi (in 1923). He later became a staunch Communist, and remained so even after Gide's *Return from the U.S.S.R.*

is one of the symbols of India and the emblem of Sri Lanka, where many elephants can still be seen, in reserves or in the wild, more than in India. In 1928, during his trip to South America, he took with him the works of Milarepa (or Milaraspa). The illustrious semi-legendary Tibetan ascetic is said to have lived in the 11th–12th centuries and to have founded a mystical sect whose two main pillars are asceticism, practised with extreme rigour, and meditation, which is at the origin of one of the three great schools of philosophy of Tibetan Buddhism, Mahâmudrâ, the 'Great Symbol'. Milarepa, who did not write down anything, is said to have transmitted his teaching orally to his disciples, in the form of discourses, songs, poems and aphorisms, piously collected by them in what became the Hundred Thousand Songs detailing the life story of the venerable Milaraspa, or, more simply, the Hundred Thousand Songs. 'A great guy,' Michaux comments familiarly.

Among his other readings, we find Kabir, another 15th century Indian mystic, whom he invoked and quoted in the epigraph at the beginning of *Un barbare en Inde* (A Barbarian in India). His 'Poems' had been translated and published by Gallimard in 1922, an event to which Gide was no stranger.

Or again Kâlidâsa, a classical Sanskrit author of the fifth century considered ancient India's greatest poet and playwright. Michaux also used to haunt the collections and the library of the Guimet Museum, before his departure and after his return. Likewise, as he gravitated towards the centre of the Gallimard galaxy, how could he not have been aware of the Galerie de la NRF, created by the Gallimard brothers and the Gallimard bookstore, associated with André Malraux, who initiated the project?

A private cultural centre, a place of exhibition, as well as for trade in works of art, the Gallery organized several important exhibitions of Asian art, in 1931–1932, each time publishing a brochure-catalogue: Gothic-Buddhist works from the Pamir, Indo-Persian sketches from the 17th to the 19th century and Indo-Hellenistic works. Perhaps Michaux went there...

Coincidence: Malraux, almost a contemporary of Michaux (he was born in 1901), pioneer of the discovery of the 'Greco-Buddhist' art of Gandhara, made his first two trips to India at that time, in the company of his wife Clara. One, a quick trip in the summer of 1930, where he just skimmed through northern India. The other, from May to November 1931, when Malraux descended through the Khyber Pass, and went down, via Delhi and Benares, to Calcutta. Within a few weeks, Michaux found them there!

According to the memories of the photographer Brassaï—another of his friends since 1925—Michaux was also passionate about yoga. He started learning Sanskrit, a language he celebrated in *Un barbare en Asie* (A Barbarian in Asia). This book constitutes our best resource on his journey, enriched and cross-checked with the documents available to literary archaeologists, notably the irreplaceable correspondence; but taking all the necessary precautions. For, as Jean-Pierre Martin, his distinguished biographer,[9] expresses well, 'HM'—as he calls him throughout his opus—is 'a barbarian of the travelogue (anti-Loti, anti-Morand)', or 'the opposite of Gide in Congo'. Well, well.

***

If we start from the principle, as Michaux's biographer apparently does, that the pages of a travelogue must be dated and geo-located, then *Un barbare en Inde* and

9 Jean-Pierre Martin, *Henri Michaux* (Paris: NRF Biographies, Gallimard, 2003).

its appendices ('Himalayan railway', *L'Inde sudionale* – 'Southern India', and 'A Barbarian in Ceylon') do not exactly fall into this genre. Unlike, in fact, in *India (without the English)* by Loti, and in *Voyage au Congo* by Gide, although the first text is much less a travel journal than the author would have us believe and the second, although written for documentary and political purposes, is one of Gide's most personal works. From the moment a writer drafts his journey after the events, and even if, like Loti, Gide, and perhaps Michaux, he takes notes on the scene, it is necessarily a subjective literary reconstruction, a work of memory with all the possible flaws, and not a photographic report. Nothing to do either with Ecuador, where, at least at the beginning, Michaux took maniacal, almost comical care in providing the reader with chronological and / or geographical references, such as: 'Hacienda Guadalupe, towards Pelileo, Ambato, 6 am. July 11', or notations like: 'The next day, off shore', like in silent films or comics.

There is no indication of dates here. As for geographical indications, they are provided, where they exist, in the course of the text. From the outset, we find ourselves thrown into the very heart of

India, in Calcutta the former capital of the British Raj, stripped of its status 20 years earlier, in favour of Delhi more 'northern' and quieter. And Michaux was to adore Calcutta, this 'city of canons', i.e., of Brahmins, where he rubs shoulder with only men—women are 'a head shorter than men', he affirmed, and 'they never go out'. He then follows up with first impressions, often accurate, even obvious—'the Indian is abundant', 'the Hindu is religious, he feels connected to everything'—and sweeping judgments: 'Never, never, will the Hindu realize to what a degree he exasperates the European'. He finds Hindi and its vowels 'silly', 'emasculated', while Bengali 'is more lyrical, the vowels are more succulent vowels and it has a sort of incense'; and he reveres Sanskrit, 'the most beautiful creation of the Indian mind, a panoramic language, admirable also to hear, contemplative, inducing introspection'. Returning at length to what strikes him the most about Calcutta, the religious aspect, the magic, the spirituality that permeates every being, everything, every action or behaviour, he compares them to the Christian religion and its temples to our cathedrals, including the one in Cologne. Sometimes jumping from rooster to donkey and from Colombo to Howrah station, Michaux clearly distinguishes, in the caste system, 'the pride of a class apart', showing in passing his empathy for the Dalits, the untouchables, pariahs outside the caste condemned to the lowest tasks—at least at the time—and whom Gandhi had made his 'children of God', his protégés. The major problems of the country are clearly visible to him: the long-standing and violent antagonism between the Hindu majority and the powerful Muslim minority, whose religion is, by nature, 'intransigent'; the colonisation by the British, which he seems to believe will last forever, the Indians being described by him as 'defeatist' and definitively subservient to the West, presented in all its gloom: 'In twenty years' time, we will care little about the Ganges!' It seems that he did not understand anything about the tremendous power of *ahimsa*, the non-violence advocated and put into practice by Gandhi, which he casually treats as a form of 'passivity'. Michaux 'loves' the Mahatma,[10] but not the Hindu intellectuals, he says, for whom he would have been only 'a passing phase'. We also note, with regard to the pujas of the Hindus, that the

10 'Great soul', a title given to Gandhi by Rabindranath Tagore.

comment: 'They are generally careful not to pray in the presence of Europeans', is not true.

Michaux sounds more accurate in Chandernagor, the French Trading Post (until 1949), located about 25 kilometres to the north of Calcutta, on the banks of the Hooghly River, which the Indians call 'the elder daughter of the Ganges' and where they bathe every day. Instead of simply recounting, or generalising, he gets involved, as if won over by the ambient sacredness, and his sentences take on the appearance of verses: 'Oh Ganges, great being, who bathes us and blesses us. Ganges, I do not describe you, I do not sketch you, I bow before you, and I make myself humble under your waves'.

As if on cue, the Western barbarian becomes a pilgrim, almost a Hindu: 'In India, if you don't pray, you have lost your way,' he affirms. It is time wasted away.

Conquered in the end by this India that 'sings' ('Do not forget that, India sings'), Michaux alternates 'things seen' in Calcutta or in the surrounding areas, such as Shantiniketan, the fief of the illustrious Rabindranath Tagore, where he founded a university and where he died in 1941. Curiously, the poet does not speak of his fellow poet, a 1913 Nobel Prize winner translated by

Gide at the NRF, and whom he had certainly read.

After Calcutta, he goes on a trip to Puri, Orissa, Darjeeling, and even as far as Madras, of which he particularly remembers the aquarium! Before concluding his text with a declaration of love for Gandhi's India, which 'is unique', and with a modest observation: Michaux is convinced that, even if he has not found it, there exists a 'Hindu personality'. It should be noted that, although he knows the distinction, he tends to equate Indian with Hindu, which perhaps explains his lack of interest in north India, in the Muslim Mughal India. Thus, if he believes that one should go to Agra, he sees the Taj Mahal as 'an excessive mausoleum', unreal, 'false in the sun. False in the moonlight...' Loti, for his part, evoked 'the most impeccable mass of white marble in the world'.

After this first long and rather erratic journey, Michaux, although he had advised the traveller against using this means of transportation (too slow according to him, considering the immensity of the country), decides to take the train, the Himalayan railway, for a small mountainous and picturesque excursion to Nepal and Tibet. In addition to the beauty of the landscapes, the traveller has fun comparing the different peoples, and noting everything that distinguishes the Hindu from his Tibetan and Nepalese brethren, who 'are the opposite' in many ways, including the way they beg. But Michaux admits to mixing everything up a bit: Ceylon and India, Darjeeling and Nepal. This second short journey will end to the sound of the long horns of Tibetan lamas, calling the faithful to prayer.

Back to India, and this time heading towards the great South, Kerala and Tamil Nadu, the Dravidian India, pre-Indo-European India, the one that Loti called 'the India of palms'. Michaux looks again carefully at the Indian languages, Malayalam and Tamil, 'agglutinative' languages that sound very different from Bengali to his ears. He notes the proliferation of deities on the façade of temples, on *gopurams*, 'bazaars for gods, demons and giants'.

He notes the sense of multitude, the propensity of Tamils to declaim, to speak loudly, to encircle the passing stranger almost to the point of suffocation. He observes their curiosity, especially about religion. Michaux is astonished by their knowledge of Jesus Christ, forgetting in passing the European colonization and the trading posts, where Christians are more numerous than elsewhere in the country. And yet, he went to Pondicherry, still French until 1954, before going to Madras, the capital of Tamil Nadu. There he goes to the theatre, and is seduced by the charm of the great actress and singer Sundarambal. And also to the cinema, it seems. Once again he notes the predisposition of Indians to the miraculous, and their supposed absence of 'critical thinking', before closing his third part of *A Barbarian in Asia* on a note of fervent praise of his Bengali friends, whom he compares, in terms of their inner life...to the English.

Presumably from Madras, before continuing his long journey to the rest of Asia at the end of February 1932, Michaux treated himself to a short trip to Ceylon, from which he brought back a few 'impressionistic' pages of *Un barbare à Ceylan* (A Barbarian in Ceylon). There is nothing remarkable, except for the slowness of the Sinhalese, some differences between the Buddhist faith (the majority) and the Hindu faith, and that of the Tamil minority.

The book, composed in a whimsical way, then offers a few pages where India is sometimes present, notably through its crows. And then, it is China.

***

Henri Michaux published *Un barbare en Asie* in January 1933, with Gallimard. He had previously sent large extracts from it to his friend Jean Paulhan, with this comment: 'This is good Michaux. It's guaranteed'. It is indeed. And the critics were not disappointed, giving the book a very warm response. The public, apparently, followed suit, since, a second edition appeared in February 1945. The text is almost the same as the first, but the author felt the need to add a very short preface. 'Twelve years separate me from this journey,' writes Michaux.

> It is there. I am here. We can't do much for each other. It was not a study and cannot become one, nor can it be further developed. Neither can it be corrected. It has lived its life. I limited myself to changing a few words and that too, only in accordance with its course.

Interesting little text, for two reasons, both in itself, and for the future of this major book by Michaux.

This approach, of constantly rereading and revisiting his texts in order to amend them, notably through the various anthologies that he would himself compose, is one of the constants of the writer's style. His main works would undergo a process of exfoliation, a peeling away of layer upon layer, leaving behind just the very essence of thought with no trace of the thinker or writer. It is as if Michaux, who endlessly strove to leave as few traces, as few imprints as possible of his earthly passage, felt his work to be a burden. He would no doubt have been embarrassed to see that it now occupies three large volumes in the Bibliothèque de la Pléiade, a 'tribute' that he refused on several occasions during his lifetime.

As for *A Barbarian in Asia*, its fate will always be a matter of concern for him, almost a remorse. He says it clearly: the book 'lived its life' in 1933, and what it recounts corresponds to a 'moment', the journey of 1931–1932, with the ideas, the culture, the preconceptions, the judgments, and the humour that were his at that point of time. But, naturally, over the years, India has evolved a great deal, and so has Michaux, who is well aware of this too.

This is why, in 1967, for its third edition, Michaux decided to intervene more forcefully. In a 'New Preface', which is more developed than the first one but whose content is the same, he expresses contrition about 'this book which no longer suits (him), which bothers (him) and offends (him), which makes him feel ashamed'. The words are very strong. Yet, at the same time, he acknowledges that 'it has a certain tone'. So what to do with it: disown it, erase it? This is what he would decide, partly, afterwards: the Barbarian would be excluded by him from his anthology *L'espace du dedans* (The Space Within), and banned from being published in paperback. He could have corrected it completely, rewritten it, but no: that would not have been appropriate, honest. Hence Michaux was satisfied with correcting 'only trifles most of the time', his interventions being indicated by a few notes marked 'n.n.' at the bottom of the page. They are few in number, but they can provide clarification, add weight to a judgement, or even make an admission of contrition. Thus, about Milarepa, Michaux rectifies: 'Bad example. He was a Tibetan.' On the subject of the Ganges, about which he had written that 'we won't care much about it in twenty years' time', he notes: 'What a mistake!' Or, towards the end of the text, when he prophesied the disappearance of the caste system 'in ten years' once 'the Hindus are in power', he corrects himself:

'Another false prediction'. And he continues: 'The revolution is yet to be effected. It will happen,' curiously enough, he refers to a book by V.S. Naipaul, *An Area of Darkness*, which he quotes. Everyone knows by now that Sir Vidia is anything but a prophet, and certainly not in the country of his ancestors. Or how, in an attempt to correct one mistake in good faith, one adds another!

As there is no such thing as chance in general, and certainly not in this case, the new edition of *Un barbare en Asie*, in the fall of 1967, follows, by a few years, an important event for Michaux: at the end of 1963, he had returned to India at the request of his friend Micheline Phankim, who had never been there. Taking advantage of the hospitality of his friend, the great writer Octavio Paz, who was then the ambassador of his country, Mexico, to India, Michaux offers the woman he loved a dream trip to Delhi and then to the rest of the country, as far south as Madras and Pondicherry.

Micheline Phankim confided to us that she still remembers Michaux's delight in strolling down Boulevard Goubert, along the Indian Ocean, in mingling with the crowd in Pondi, colourful, mixed, and multi-religious (Hindus, Christians, Muslims…). After that, Micheline returned to France and Michaux would wander alone to Rajasthan. Naturally, it was a shock: he was well aware that India, which had been independent since 1947, had changed a great deal, even if he would still find its age-old foundations there. He had been told so, especially by his close Indian friends: the poet and translator Lokenath Bhattacharya, married to France, professor of Bengali at the Langues-O and translator; or Krishna Kripalani-Riboud, Tagore's grand-niece and wife of the industrialist Jean. Well, two Bengalis... Michaux was to express his admiration for Lokenath by dedicating to him the poem *Fille de la montagne* (Daughter of the mountain):

> *Beauty as knowledge*
> *a higher degree of knowledge.*

In the same way, he would evoke his friend Krishna in a very beautiful text, *En Occident le jardin d'une femme indienne* (In the West the Garden of an Indian Woman), that he seems to have mulled over for a long time, and reworked a lot. Thus, in one of his versions, it reads:

'Krishna R. in this unique garden makes us forget the city, Europe, the era'.[11]

We can consider that, thanks to this second trip, he had made peace with India, which is attested to by his 'new notes' at the bottom of the pages of the *Barbarian*, even though he would continue to treat this book in a special way, almost ostracising it. As for the country, it would never cease to fascinate him until his death. The poet and publisher André Velter, who was a friend of his, testifies that towards the end of his life, Michaux, when he no longer liked to receive visitors and preferred the telephone, greatly enjoyed it when Velter called him to give him news of India, and of his travels.

Conversations between barbarians, for 'Here, barbarians we were, barbarians we must remain'? In fact, Michaux had become one of the finest connoisseurs of Asia in general, and of India in particular, and was extremely familiar with all oriental wisdom. In 1970, steeped in this universe, he published 'Yantra',[12]

11 Text that remained unpublished at the time of Michaux's death, published in the journal *L'ire des vents* (The Wrath of the Wind) in February 1985.

12 Henri Michaux, *Le Point Cardinal*, 1970, reprinted in *Moments: traversées du temps* (Paris: Gallimard, 1973).

a rather abstruse metaphysical poem, intended to accompany the Tantric Art exhibition held at the Point Cardinal, the gallery where he himself used to exhibit his recent paintings and drawings every year:

The cloud of being condenses
folds up
Cosmos-Universe
cosmos of the universe of the 'self'.

In 40 years, the so-called barbarian had learned a lot.

IV

Tamil Nadu, Sri Lanka
The Domain of Gods

André Malraux, in the long preface that he wrote for *Les Cahiers de la Petite Dame*[13]—a text that is as fundamental as it is little known—in which Maria Van Rysselberghe became André Gide's impeccable memoirist from 1918 to 1951, notes this sentence by their common friend: 'I am quite resistant to India; its dizzying quality has an opposite effect on me.' Was Gide too Protestant by education to succumb to the Indian furia? Too monotheistic, in any case, to venture into this truly vertiginous Hindu pantheon. India, as Michaux perceived well, is a gigantic temple-land, which can, like the country itself, fascinate or repel.

What seduced me immediately and made me feel deliciously disoriented in the Hindu religion is its

13 André Malraux, *Les Cahiers de la Petite Dame*, Volume 1, 1918-1929, (Paris: Gallimard, 1973).

sheer profusion. One or two million gods, who knows? All categories combined, from the most revered 'big bosses' like Brahma, Siva, Vishnu, Krishna, Parvati, Kali, Ganesh and so on, to the most obscure, small local deities who, at times, don't even have a name, but who are nonetheless venerated with equal fervour.

In India, Hinduism, brought into their fold by the Aryan invaders, is 'more than a religion, it is an identity, a way of life, the result of more than 4,000 years of human intellectual activity', writes Nigel Hankin in his *Hanklyn-Janklin*,[14] the most valuable work, part encyclopaedia, part dictionary, and part finely analytical essay, for anyone who wants to understand something about the country, its people, and their languages. Without a sacred book, without a supreme leader, Hinduism, practised by the vast majority of the population (about 80%), was grafted onto the pre-existing pagan substratum. And in its worship, especially in the countryside and in the Dravidian south—whose populations, indigenous or those who had arrived much earlier, according to opposing theories, preceded the Aryans—there

14 Nigel B. Hankin, *Hanklyn-Janklin* (New Delhi: India Research Press, 2003).

remains, obvious traces of animism. 'The Hindu has idolatry in his skin', wrote Michaux.[15]

I am, like so many other Westerners, a lukewarm Catholic. I have been through the whole process: baptism, communion, even confirmation, to please my family and because at the time (late 1960s, early 1970s) everybody followed the same course—all my high school friends, except for the Protestants (of whom I didn't know any), and Jews. I knew a lot of them then. I did all my secondary schooling at the Lycée Charlemagne, in the heart of the Marais, a few blocks from the Rue des Rosiers. On Jewish holidays, the class was cut by a good third, and my friends Boralevi, Choukroun or Cohen would recount to us, the next day, about the ceremonies in which they had taken part. This exoticism already appealed to on me, especially as my own religion, reformed by the Second Vatican Council, had seen its liturgy washed out, secularised and translated into French. Farewell, obscurity, mystery, pomp, incense and prayers in Latin! And, 'without Latin, without Latin, the Mass bores us', sang, I believe, the very free-thinking Georges Brassens.

15 In *Un barbare en Asie*, of course.

I am an aesthetic Catholic, a traditionalist agnostic, a Gidean, respectful of all religions on condition that none are imposed on him. Wherever I find myself and whatever the denomination, I love nothing more than to enter all places of worship, churches when they are open, mosques when one is permitted, synagogues, temples—temples, particularly—preferably when a ceremony is taking place there, and to communicate with the faithful, sincerely, even if I don't believe in anything that brings them together. The fervour always impresses me, even if, deep down, I retain my own personal space, my ideas, and my secular values.

That is to say that when I am in India, in this domain of the gods, in this immense open-air temple, I am overwhelmed. During all these years, when I have travelled to India, several tens of times, almost everywhere, I have visited an incalculable number of temples, both grandiose and modest, and I don't know how many *pujas* I have done, guided by a friend or an anonymous believer, a fellow devotee who is delighted to help the foreigner, to show him the beauty of his faith. Even in Paris, I went to fulfil my duties to Ganesh, in his little temple beyond Little

India and the Boulevard de la Chapelle, very difficult to locate in a neighbourhood that was undergoing construction at the time.

I particularly like the contrast in Hinduism between the infinitely complex and sophisticated liturgy and rituals and the simple, individual practice. Every Hindu prays to his god face-to-face, at home or in the temple, alone or with the help of a priest. Puja quickly completed, offerings, small gifts exchanged, the forehead marked with sacred ashes, different according to the chosen god, then a return to normal routine, not without a certain sense of pride in of having demonstrated his piety. Of course, there are also great festivals with bells, processions and pilgrimages, of which the Indians are particularly fond. But there is no obligation to participate. Nirvana cannot be earned in this way.

Striking, also, is this contrast between a religion that advocates the finest of human values, and the violence that lurks underneath. But isn't this the case with all religions, even apparently the most peaceful and seemingly non-confrontational ones, when they have the wind in their sails, or when they feel threatened by another?

***

In the summer of 2013, after nearly four years of missing India, I wanted to follow a sort of cure: a month of total immersion in a small village in the state of Pondicherry. Alternating between secular life: walks in Pondi, meeting up with French and Indian friends who live there, a weekend of idleness in Tranquebar, a former Danish trading post not far from Karaikal, a former French trading post, and a visit to the modest 'museum' in Kizhor, not far from where I live, and where the deed of restitution by France of its trading posts to the Republic of India was signed on 18 October 1954...; And the 'sacred' life: visiting all the temples, large or barely existent, well-known or obscure, where my Indian guide and friend Desikhan would take me. He is a rather astonishing boy, in his 30s.

Small, thin and nervous like many Tamils, lively and resourceful, Desikhan is the assistant of Ulrike, a German anthropologist friend from the University of Dortmund, married to a Tamil, who has perfectly integrated into the village and the local way of life, and has been working and living in the area for decades. I didn't quite understand what her research was about, but thanks to her, Desikhan, her appointed driver, knows like the back of his hand, a state that is vast (130,000 km^2), more populated than France, criss-crossed by 200,000 kilometres of roads, both surfaced and un-surfaced. Desikhan, in order to make ends meet and to feed his wife and children (two – a girl and a boy – both very well brought up), has set up a micro-travel agency. He drives around Ulrike's students when they come to do fieldwork, and some tourists, the happy few, friends of friends, like me. In addition to his qualities as a driver and guide, Desikhan, a Hindu and a fundamentalist – not devoid of a certain distance and humour with regard to his religion – was happy to show me as many temples as possible, giving me the necessary historical explanations for each one, but also initiating me into the rites, which we practiced together. He, really praying, and I, participating and observing, in total empathy.

We had, in our broken 'bazaar' English (it doesn't matter, with the vast majority of Indians, we always understand each other) long conversations, sometimes animated, where I would either willingly play the naïve, or exert the traits of the rationalistic Westerner. My favourite joke: 'Hinduism is an expensive religion',

I used to tell him, when, at the end of the day, we had emptied our pockets of all the 10, 50 or 100 rupee notes we had taken with us in the morning for the offerings. In the temples, one pays everywhere. Each puja is accompanied by a small note, slipped discreetly into a tray, or into the hand of the priest, who is generally smiling and well fed. Once, even, I don't remember where but I did take a picture of a Brahmin accepting a credit card! It was like being in one of our monastic shops, like at La Trappe. This made Desikhan laugh a lot, and he nodded in agreement, his pockets as empty as mine. I spared him the Marxist discourse on the 'opium of the people' and the exploitation of human credulity for commercial purposes.

In this context, the crowning glory is undoubtedly the Sripuram of Vellore, in the far east of Tamil Nadu, not far from Andhra Pradesh. The Sri Lakshmi Narayani Golden Temple is a vast private religious complex, founded and managed by the Sri Narayani Peedam trust, headed by a young billionaire Sri Sakthi Narayani Amma, as pious as he is wise, who lives not far from there, in his very Bollywood-like estate. This does not prevent him from performing ceremonies in person in his temple, which lies at the end of a very well-marked route, lined with numerous shops selling expensive religious trinkets, which the pilgrim is obliged to pass through. One pays an entrance fee of 500 rupees—a large sum for a 'basic' Indian—for a special 'skip-the-line' access to the heart of the shrine: a solid gold statue of the goddess Lakshmi, 'donated' by Sri Sakthi Narayani Amma. Seventy kilos of glittering prosperity in a small, fully gilded temple, in the middle of an oval pond, at the very centre of a six-pointed star where one walks along impeccably maintained gardens and water features. Mr Narayani must command an army of gardeners. Photos are not allowed, but after the puja, the VIP, who has already been relieved of a 500 rupee deposit (not counting the deposits for shoes, camera, the obligatory purchase of a *veshti* if you are wearing Bermuda shorts, which was my case: Desikhan had a lot of fun dressing me up as a Tamil) is offered a small, very baba-cool plastic coated canvas bag, adorned with a colourful image of the revered Guru, seated on a giant pink lotus flower, blessing the faithful. Inside, one finds a few small gifts: a sweet, a brochure about the temple, an orange cotton cord that Hindus tie on their right wrist....Even my very religious friend had to acknowledge the excess, the kitsch and commercial aspect of all this, worthy of Disneyland.

The piety of the Hindus is tangible. It is manifested in countless statues and sacred objects, before which the believer makes a sign and murmurs a short prayer. In the domain of the gods, the sacred is present at every moment, at every step. I had thus observed that Desikhan never passed a temple or a statue without respecting this ritual. One day, we visited the Tanjore Museum together (Thanjavur in Tamil, once one of the capitals of the Chola Empire), located in the former palace of the Maharajah. In the different rooms, there were mainly bronze statues of gods and goddesses from the Chola period (whose peak was from the ninth to the 13th centuries AD), Desikhan passed in front of them seemingly unmoved, like any foreign tourist. I was astonished: what is the difference between these statues and those in the temples? His response was sublime: 'A god is a statue before which one prays'.

In his own way, he solved Malraux's great question regarding art and the sacred: at what point does an object of worship become a work of art and, on entering a museum, does it lose its religious significance, its magic? The answer lies in the attitude of the man. If, as a visitor, he only admires, the work is 'disembodied', secular. But if, as a pilgrim, he prays, then the object regains all its power, its primary meaning.

As soon as we stepped out into the courtyard of the Tanjore Museum, Desikhan hurried to say a quick prayer in front of a small altar to Ganesh, all glistening with ghee and in front of which was burning a stick of incense, all the pleasant perfume entering the divine trunk.

Sometimes we had more heated, political discussions. A committed Hindu, Desikhan is an activist for the BJP, the Hindu fundamentalist and nationalist Bharatiya Janata Party, which once governed the country in the 2000s and is reportedly poised to return to power in the legislative elections of spring 2014.[16] Like most Westerners, nourished in addition, by my reading and my association with Malraux, I tend to favour the secular and more 'left-wing' Congress Party, the old party of Gandhi and Nehru, the one that contributed to the liberation and

16 **Editor's note:** The BJP and its alliance partners in a coalition called the National Democratic Alliance (NDA) won the Indian general elections in 2014. After the five-year term of the NDA government was over, they won the general elections in 2019. The next general elections are likely to be held in 2024.

founding of the modern and democratic India. Which Desikhan hates, accusing it of having done nothing for the people, and of being totally corrupt. These are the two most common criticisms of governments in India, a country whose political life is about as simple as the Hindu pantheon! On the subject of corruption, I reminded him that his friends, when Mr Vajpayee was Prime Minister, had been caught red-handed taking bribes by *Tehelka,* the courageous magazine created by the journalist-writer Tarun Tejpal. As for the assessment of politicians, we French are well placed to know that they are made to say almost everything and also its exact opposite. Questions of perspective, of ideology, even of propaganda: 'Truth below the Pyrenees, error beyond', said Montaigne. Our friendly jousting, interspersed with a few silences, music (Tamil or Beatles, depending on who was in charge), countless phone calls—Desikhan is a compulsive mobile phone addict, even when driving, which I protested against as much as I could, even going so far as to confiscate, with a smile, the object of the crime—allowed us to pleasantly fill the hundreds of hours we spent together on the roads of Tamil Nadu, 'surfaced' or 'un-surfaced', but always insane, bottle-necked, diverted (due to end-of-monsoon floods, road-works, landslides, accidents...) and dreadfully slow. One day, it took us 11 hours from our village to Tanjore and back, just to spend two or three hours there. Desikhan was exhausted. But never, even while driving at night, a particularly perilous exercise in India, was his vigilance in question. At no time did I feel myself to be in danger. Perhaps I was wrong. But Ganesh has always protected me. My devotion to the little elephant God, the son of Siva and Parvati, greatly pleased my Hindu friend, who one day gave me a statue of my favourite God. For my part, having questioned him about his own preference, I presented him with a statue of Murugan, his favourite. Murugan is the brother of Ganesh. In India, chance does not exist.

So, that summer, I visited and revisited a multitude of temples. It is like a divine kaleidoscope that makes you dizzy, but does not bore you, unlike Pharaonic Egypt, with its repetitive and rigid splendours. 'Seen from Ellora,' notes Malraux in his *Antimémoires*, 'Egypt seemed like an austere and geometric India'. In India, temples are alive, they are in fact at the heart of life. And of death.

Like this Alakar Temple, whose open-air altar is surrounded by a host of small multi-coloured statues representing all the deceased inhabitants of the village, with their animals and familiar objects, as a kind of votive offering. A poignant collection of bric-à-brac somewhat reminiscent of the palace of the Facteur Cheval. Or the Banyan Tree Temple in Sivaranthagam, one of the most magical places I know. Here again, the very modest altar is in the open air, facing a huge, centuries-old banyan tree, the main trunk of which is hollowed out with several cavities. We pray there, we make offerings to the powerful God Vishnu, 'fighter of good against evil, protector of the world' (says Hankin) symbolized by the cobra Ananta (or Shesha). Snakes abound in the area, and the sacred tree is said to harbour them. We did not see any during our visit. On another day, however, as we wandered through half-flooded rice fields in search of another temple, a long snake practically slithered under our bare feet.

The Banyan Tree Temple is served by a rather impressive old priestess, who looks like a sorceress with her bedraggled hair and filthy clothes. In Dravidian country, where the Brahmins arrived only later, a woman can be a priest, and a non-Brahmin too.

Though it is undoubtedly the son of the 'sorceress', charming and 'clean', who will take over the priestly functions. A future well mapped out. That said, the priestess is a friendly and talkative person. She made us participate in a long puja and enjoyed explaining the myths and rites of her duties. I was told that a scene from Ang Lee's film *Life of Pi* was shot here.

We visited sublime Chola temples, such as the Thirukunthankudi Mahadevar Temple in Madagadipet (11th century), or the temple built by Rajendra Chola I in Gangaikonda Cholapuram, a rural site where hundreds of schoolchildren had been taken that day by their teachers. I adore Indian schoolchildren, with their impeccable uniforms, ties for boys and girls, their neatly combed and well-oiled hair, their (momentary) discipline, their bright smiles, imbued with a measure of gravity. We also saw many temples dedicated to Shiva, one of the most celebrated gods in Tamil Nadu, in Tiruvandarkoil, Villianur or even the more modest one in Bahour.

These signs of the purest animism, which the layman does not necessarily notice unless he is accompanied by an Indian who explains to him their significance, are very striking and almost everywhere:

stones simply placed along a road, pieces of cloth or plastic bags filled with indefinable objects hanging from trees, palm branches hung on a house under construction, so many signs, all propitiatory votive offerings. Polymorphic polytheists, pagans by nature and by tradition, for the Hindus everything is God, everything is sacred. Especially for the Jains, a particular branch of Hinduism, who respect all forms of life with a fanatical scrupulousness. Desikhan took us to a rare Jain cave temple not far from Gingee, with a stunning view of the two forts, Rani Fort on the left, Rajah Fort on the right. That day, it had rained, and our brave Tata Nano, a worthy emulator of Nicolas Bouvier's Fiat Topolino, displayed a lot of grit by driving us to the bottom of the cliff, along narrow, rutted and soggy paths. But nothing stops Desikhan. Not even the acrobatic ascent of the hill-temple, nor the hundreds of chaotic steps of the fortress of Gingee.

Some temples are cities within cities, such as the Rajarajeswaram in Tanjore, which would require a whole day to visit. Which is impossible, unless you are a priest. The temples are not open all day, and worshippers are usually only allowed in early in the morning, and from mid-afternoon onwards, though with fairly flexible schedules. When you come from far away, it is better to be patient. But what would one not do to enjoy a private audience with Siva, Parvati or Ganesh?

In the temples, time seems to have stood still, such as in Chidambaram, one of the largest and the most majestic, where I thought I had found the same 'brahmes' as had my master Loti. Young and handsome, with an immaculate *veshti,* sacred thread crossing their 'bronze' torsos, big smouldering eyes that stare at you with a palpable arrogance and a sense of superiority, but all smiles and grace, with their long silky hair swept up on the nape of their necks in a sophisticated bun.

Frozen for eternity, too, are the ruins of Fort Nawab of Arcot or the two citadels of Gingee. Sublime witnesses to the fierce battles fought, from the 17th century, between the French and the English, allied to this or that maharajah, rajah, nawab or nizam, for the domination of a part of the immense country and its wealth, real or legendary. The treasures of Golconda, of course, could only be Indian. But the immense fortress of Quli Qutb Shah, not far from Hyderabad, in Andhra Pradesh, which Loti visited, is a dead city.

It inspired him to write some beautiful pages, full of that 'strange and nostalgic charm'[17] which is one of his favourite themes. Loti was a great melancholic. Even without being so, how can one not be impressed by these abandoned cities of which there are so many in India. The most beautiful and the most memorable of them is undoubtedly Fatehpur Sikri, very close to Agra, in Uttar Pradesh, the short-lived capital of the Mughal Akbar. Founded in 1569, it did not survive the emperor, abandoned definitively in 1605, we don't know for what reasons. *Sic transit gloria mundi ...*

***

I had waited to go to Sri Lanka (no longer called Ceylon since 1972) until the end of the merciless civil war that had been waged there since the 1980s between the Sinhalese government, which is Buddhist, and the Tamil minority, which is Hindu. Under the British colonial rule, forced cohabitation was the rule. After independence and the republic, the latent conflict between the dominant majority (about 70%) and the discriminated minority (about 20%) degenerated into

17 *India (without the English)*, Book V, Chapter III, op. cit.

a bitter struggle on both sides, with the same abuses, and massacres of innocent civilians. Led by the most radical elements of their community, the Marxist Tigers of the LTTE (Liberation Tigers of Tamil Eelam), the Tamils, originally from southern India but settled on the opposite island for generations, demanded the creation of an independent state, to the north and east, with Jaffna as its capital. This failed. The Tigers were defeated, the repression was fierce, and an armed peace was signed in 2002, under the aegis of Norway.

So I went there in the summer of 2003. I was delighted to finally discover this miniature India, more peaceful, apparently calmer, perhaps due to the combined effects of Buddhism, which in principle advocates non-violence, the *Ahimsa* of Mahatma Gandhi, and certainly too, a higher standard of living. In addition to the beauty of the country, the richness of its natural and cultural heritage, the infinite kindness of its inhabitants, Sinhalese and Tamils mixed together—though I stayed in the south and in the centre, the north not being accessible—I was struck by this harmony between the two religions, which sometimes bordered on syncretism. In almost all the shrines dedicated to Buddha—the reclining Buddha, the Buddha-mountain inside which the pilgrim can walk... — one can find small altars dedicated to the most popular Hindu gods: my friend Ganesh, in particular, has crossed the Palk Strait, which separates India from Sri Lanka, and the elephant has become the symbol of the island.

During the Perahera, the great festival that takes place at the end of July in Kandy — the former capital of the Sinhalese kingdom until the 19th century and a sacred city for Buddhists with its Temple of the Tooth of Buddha — the procession of sumptuously caparisoned elephants mounted by the rajahs who own them, also includes performances by Hindu dance schools. Yellow and saffron costumes, thunderous music and exuberant figures contrast with the placid dignity of the pachyderms, and their senator-like steps.

Culturally, Sri Lanka has been part of the Indian sphere since its origin. The island was conquered by the Cholas. And one of the most famous episodes of the *Ramayana* takes place there. My memories of my stay in Sri Lanka were enchanting, despite the myriads of relentless mosquitoes that devoured me, day and night. I stayed there longer than Loti, criss-crossing the country, the coastlines and tea plantations, the elephant reserves, Kandy and Galle, were all sublime. I had plenty of time: I was not an academician; no maharajah was waiting for me in Travancore....This paradisiacal harmony was put to the test, barely a few months after my return, by the tsunami at the end of 2003, the most violent in decades, which also hit part of the Indian coast very hard, in Andhra Pradesh and Tamil Nadu. In Vailankanni, in particular, the vast Catholic shrine south of the Bay of Bengal, several thousands of pilgrims who had come to celebrate Christmas and were sleeping on the beach were overwhelmed by the raging waves.

Life has since resumed. But so has violence: I recently read in a newspaper that in Sri Lanka, 'the Muslim and the Christian minority are the targets of attacks by an extremist Buddhist group, the Bodu Bala Sena (BBS). The organization is part of a larger radical movement that is spreading dangerously across Southeast Asia.'[18]

18 *Le Figaro*, 20 January 2014.

V

André Malraux's Temptation of India

We still find ourselves dreaming of the great Indian novel that André Malraux could have written, when he was writing novels ranging from the *Conquérants* (Conquerors, 1928) to the *Noyers de l'Altenburg* (The Walnut Trees of Altenburg, 1948). Why not, after the insurgent China of *La Condition Humane* (Man's Fate, 1933) and Spain at war in *L'espoir* (Man's Hope, 1937), to celebrate and stage, for example, the independence of India on 15 August 1947?

But in 1947, Malraux was fighting another battle, Franco-French, as the propaganda delegate of the R.P.F. (Rassemblement du Peuple Français—Rally of the French People), the Gaullist party. Two years earlier, he had even been Minister of Information in General de Gaulle's short-lived government of National Unity. And then there was the father of Indian freedom,

Mahatma Gandhi, whom Malraux never met, and with whom he had less affinity than he had with the Chinese revolutionaries, or the Spanish Republicans. Or even, with Gandhi's right-hand man and political son, Pandit Nehru. Gandhi was too mystical for the agnostic Malraux, who was much more comfortable with a pragmatic, Marxist statesman who, in addition, was an atheist, rejecting the traditional notion of God, as Nehru wrote in his autobiography.[19]

And why, when Malraux stopped writing novels to refocus his creativity on art, history or literature, did he not devote a definitive artistic, spiritual and prophetic essay to India? It must be noted that these books do not exist.

Paradoxically, India is without doubt the distant country which Malraux visited most often: in 1930–1931—and not in 1929 as he wrote in his *Antimémoires*[20]—1958, 1965, 1973, until his last trip in the end of 1974, which sounded like a farewell. It is the oriental civilisation that has attracted him the most, since his youth, when he attended (as a dilettante) Sanskrit classes at the Langues-O and (more

19 Jawaharlal Nehru, *The Discovery of India* (Arles: Philippe Piquier, 2002).

20 André Malraux, *Antimémoires* (Paris: Gallimard, 1967).

assiduously, it seems) the collections of the Musée Guimet. An agnostic fascinated by a country so deeply spiritual, which was built on a religion, Hinduism (later its avatar Buddhism), an aesthete fascinated by a multi-millennial art that he integrated into the vast cycle of his *La Métamorphose des dieux*[21] (The Metamorphosis of the Gods), a man committed to the history of his century, fascinated by an immense nation that was shaking off the British colonial yoke by practising Gandhian non-violence, achieving its independence, then steadily gaining its place among the great emerging countries (which, from the 1950s onwards, were called the 'non-aligned' nations), Malraux, in his last years, insisted on the major role that India would be called upon to play one day on the world stage. A few fools had sneered at him then, yet doesn't the beginning of the third millennium prove him a little more right every day?

Through the intermediary of intellectuals and writers who passed on culture, wisdom or Indian literature (such as Gurdjieff,[22] Romain Rolland, and

21 André Malraux, *La Métamorphose des Dieux*, (Paris: Gallimard, 1957), completely revised in three volumes, published from 1974 to 1977.

22 Georges Ivanovitch Gurdjieff (1877-1949), a Russian thinker living in France who, in his 'method', tried to mix Far Eastern wisdom with Western esotericism.

his friend André Gide), Malraux had read Tagore and the great sacred texts. He admired Gandhi, and was impressed by this revolutionary who had never had blood on his hands, even if many atrocities were committed in his name and for the cause he embodied, during the terrible Partition in 1947 with Pakistan. From 1936, the date of their first real meeting in Paris, it was thanks to Jean Guéhenno that Malraux maintained ties of close friendship and understanding with Nehru until his death in 1964. When one was Minister of State and the other the first Prime Minister of free India, they deepened their dialogue on world order at the highest intellectual, moral and philosophical level. This privileged relationship continued with Indira Gandhi, Nehru's daughter and political heiress, 'programmed' by him for struggle and the exercise of power, beside whom Malraux physically engaged in 1971 during the Indo-Pakistan war, which led to the independence of Bangladesh.

'André loved India,' wrote Sophie de Vilmorin, the last woman in Malraux's life, who accompanied him on several of his trips, in *Aimer encore.*[23] Particularly about his trip of 1974 when, aged, ill and tired,

23 Sophie de Vilmorin, *Aimer Encore* (Paris: Gallimard, 1999).

he felt the need to make a last tour of India, a final pilgrimage, to see once more his beloved temples of Ajanta and Ellora, and the caves of Elephanta, before he died. '(From India),' continues his companion-memoirist, 'he knew all the gods, all the philosophies, all the transcendent expressions.' Of India, he knew a lot, and understood everything. In India, he travelled a lot. On India, he spoke a lot, worked quite a bit. However, he did not write much, except in the *Antimémoires* (Anti-Memoirs). Yet India, with whom he had such a unique relationship, irrigated, nourished and 'metamorphosed' his entire existence, his thought and his work.

One of André Malraux's earliest and little known literary projects—its composition underwent a complex and singular process, its publication appearing only in six fragments and in reviews, and its title changed several times—was originally entitled *Écrit pour une idole à trompe* (Written for an Idol with a Trunk). Malraux had started writing it in early 1921, the same year that his first real book, *Lunes en papier* (Paper Moons), appeared. The work brings together three tales that flirt with the fantastic: *Les Hérissons apprivoisés* (Tamed Hedgehogs), *Journal d'un pompier du Jeu de massacre* (Diary of a Fireman from the Game of Massacre) and *Écrit pour un ours en peluche* (Written for a Teddy Bear). Three texts of youth, of extreme youth, dedicated to Ganesh, the elephant-headed Hindu god, as a totem. But in these pages, apart from an insignificant allusion to a fire in Bengal, there is nothing Indian. On the other hand, there is already an indication of a curiosity for the Orient on the part of a Malraux perfectly in tune with his time.

The 1920s, in France and in Europe, were marked, for a certain number of young intellectuals, by a desire to forget, to break away after the world conflict of 1914–1918, in which they had not, for the most part, directly participated, but which had deeply traumatised them. An awareness of the horrors of war, which André Breton and Louis Aragon, for example, would denounce. A 'Never again' that made its way into people's minds. At the same time, the war, with the involvement of tens of thousands of soldiers from all parts of what was then called the 'French Empire', accelerated, among these same intellectuals, a process of critical reflexion on our colonial system.

Malraux, in 1921, was 20 years old. And he was, in his own way, an intellectual. Even if he had only briefly passed through the mould of official education: in 1918, rejected at the Lycée Condorcet, he abandoned his secondary studies. As a self-taught man, he acquired extensive knowledge. And as for oriental culture: it was at the École des Langues Orientales and the Guimet Museum. More than anything else, he was an obsessive reader. A brilliant young man blessed with an immense appetite for knowledge and discovery. 'Culture is not inherited, it is acquired' was his motto. An astonishing intellectual machine who impressed his listeners, as Gide would later testify on several occasions, with humility and not without humour:

> Like Valéry, Andre Malraux's great strength is his indifference to whether the listener is tired, bored or lost, especially if the listener (like me) pretends rather than truly follows his words. That is why any conversation with these two friends remains, for me at least, somewhat mortifying, and I emerge from it more overwhelmed than elated.

To entitle one of his first books, *Écrit pour une idol à trompe* (Written for an Idol with a Trunk) was, from the start of his literary career, to manifest a 'temptation of the Orient'. It was a desire to discover other civilisations, other philosophies, to put our Judeo-Christian heritage on hold. Yet, at the same time, to also express a certain rejection of Western culture—as Loti, 60 years older than Malraux, had done before him. It is the very opposite of a whole bourgeois and conventional literature, the one against which the NRF of Gide and his friends would be formed. This attitude was accentuated by Malraux's taste for what he called the 'eccentric', a word and a tendency that would remain with him throughout his life. The eccentric was Malraux's favourite form of humour, a dimension that his critics and biographers have not always sufficiently taken into account. Did he not publish later, in 1928, that is to say between *Les Conquérants* (The Conquerors) and *La Voie Royale* (The Royal Way), at Gallimard, a limited edition book (572 copies), aptly titled *Royaume-Farfelu* (The Kingdom of Farfelu), he himself calling it 'literary cubism'? In Malraux's work we find skeletons that roller-skate; fish that come out of the water wearing spectacles...a fantasy not far removed from that of Lewis Carroll in *Alice in Wonderland*, or that of the first poems of Henri Michaux.

Ganesh could then have appeared exotic to the general public. Not so to a section of the intelligentsia who, for some time now, had been interested in India and its thought. In addition to specialists such as Grousset and Guénon,[24] even Maurice Barrès was impressed by Indian spirituality, despite being so 'rooted', he dreamt of an 'elsewhere', an Orient more poetic than real. André Gide, as early as 1913, translated Rabindranath Tagore's *L'Offrande lyrique,* while confiding, in 1918: 'But this Oriental in India isn't made to suit me.' Or again, 'I am quite resistant to India; its quality of dizziness has the opposite effect on me.'

Tagore, who, in 1921, came to Paris to give a lecture, was rather coldly received by the public. The man was not always easy to deal with....Let us also recall the biographies of Ramakrishna and Gandhi, written by Romain Rolland.

From 1927 onwards, there was also an avant-garde movement, less famous than Dada, less enduring than

24 René Guénon (1886–1981), philosopher who turned his life into a long metaphysical quest. He was interested for a time in Hinduism (*L'Homme et son devenir selon le Vêdânta,* Man and his Future according to the Vedanta, 1925) before converting to Islam in Egypt, where he lived from 1930 and later died.

surrealism, but nevertheless fundamental: Le Grand Jeu, by René Daumal[25] and Roger Gilbert-Lecomte. The only one to take a close interest in metaphysics and, through the writings of Gurdjieff, to assume a spiritual dimension, nourished by references to India. Michaux, for a time, was close to the *Grand Jeu* (The Great Game). In 1934 he even participated in the publication of the fourth issue of its eponymous review, which never saw light of day.

Malraux, who from 1921 onwards was evolving in Parisian literary circles, reading Gide and the NRF, and starting to work in publishing, was necessarily aware of these individual or collective approaches, of these various publications. That year was important for him, as after his marriage to Clara Goldschmidt, he would begin to travel, first in Europe, then further and further afield. And, from 1923, in Indochina. From then on, until the mid-1930s, the writer was to be one of the few to focus his work on the Orient, which

25 René Daumal (1908–1944), poet for whom literature was inseparable from mystical research. He studied Sanskrit and the teachings of Gurdjieff, who was his teacher, and spent time in the United States with the troupe of Uday Shankar, Ravi's uncle. 'Le Grand Jeu', a review and movement founded in 1928 with Roger Gilbert-Lecomte and Roger Vailland, is one of the only European avant-garde movements to have integrated the spiritual dimension into its research.

he visited to a greater or lesser extent, sometimes imagining, always transforming. To take into account an immense part of the world that until then had been confined almost exclusively to travelogues for lovers of exoticism, to stage a dialogue between different cultures. To feel these tensions, these revolts born of oppression and racism, which would soon shake the colonial world. And to bear witness, whether lived or recreated, it mattered little: with Malraux, what was not yet called the Third World made its entry into literature, through the front door.

His travels, his personal adventures or misadventures, such as the affair of the looting of the Banteay Srey temple in Cambodia in 1923, or his first political struggle in 1925 with his newspapers *Indochine* and *L'Indochine enchaînée,* would all contribute to his work. In 1926, *La Tentation de l'Occident* (The Temptation of the West) would see a young Chinese intellectual in dialogue with his French counterpart. *Les Conquérants* (The Conquerors, 1928) and *La Condition humaine* (Man's Fate, 1933) showed a China in the grip of its first revolutionary convulsions. While *La Voie Royale* (The Way of the Kings, 1930) would transpose the Cambodian hold-up into a novel....The epic story of Malraux as a revolutionary leader and fellow traveller of communism is in the process of being born.

Malraux left for the Orient for the first time in 1930, with a stopover in Afghanistan, in search of works of Greco-Buddhist art, of which he would organize an exhibition at the Galérie de la NRF in January 1931. Then, during a sort of dizzying world tour that lasted from May to December of the same year, he finally discovered India: Delhi, Benares, Calcutta. All the while working on *La Condition humaine*. His last adventure, oriental and eccentric, would be in 1934, the expedition, with his lifelong accomplice Louis Corniglion-Molinier, in search of the capital of the Queen of Sheba....The end of Malraux's 'oriental' youth. Of his youth altogether. From the middle of the 1930s, the urgency lay elsewhere. In 1935, Mussolini's fascist Italy invaded Ethiopia. It was anything but a charade, as it has often been portrayed: the Italian troops committed exactions and massacres, and used gas. And André Malraux was one of the few intellectuals to protest. Hitler, Chancellor since 1933, was chomping at the bit. Franco sharpened his bayonets. For Malraux, it was no longer a time for petitions and commitment through writing, but for combat. This would be followed by political action.

And one would have to wait for his books on art of the 1950s, then, above all, his *Antimemoires* in 1967, for the Orient—and India—to reappear in his writings. And that, coming full circle, an elephant emerges from his Buddhist text, as an epigraph to the *Antimémoires*, to offer its trunk to the Ganesh of 1921: 'The elephant is the wisest of all animals, the only one that remembers its previous lives; so he holds himself still for a long time, meditating on them'.

Even if the *Antimémoires*, as their name indicates, take pains to disrupt the chronology and blur the tracks, it is now possible to reconstruct the various journeys that Malraux made to India, and their impact on his life, his work, his political commitments and his writings. After his first 'contacts' in 1930 and 1931, Malraux's destiny made him wait until 1958 to bring him back to India. From 27 November to 7 December, the writer, appointed by General de Gaulle, upon his return to power, as Minister Delegate to the Presidency of the Council, in charge of Information, was sent on a mission to Iran, India and Japan. The trip to India was preceded by a message from the

General to Prime Minister Nehru. Today, in India, these gestures of friendship have not been forgotten, the foundations of a special bond that continues to exist with France. Thus, in 2003, Her Excellency Sheila Dikshit, Chief Minister of Delhi, and His Excellency Dominique Girard, Ambassador of France to India, named a part of an avenue André Malraux Marg, unveiling a commemorative plaque recalling his interest in India. Perpendicular to the very chic Shanti Path, the Avenue Foch of Delhi, André Malraux Marg separates the French Embassy from the American one! And Malraux was at the time the only foreign writer honoured in the Indian capital, along with Tolstoy.

Arriving in Delhi on 27 November 1958 and received with full honours, Malraux had a long interview with the Indian Prime Minister the next day, at his residence, in the presence of Count Stanislas Ostrorog, French Ambassador to India and a knowledgeable expert on the country. Ostrorog, in accordance with the bureaucratic norms, took notes during the meeting, which were used for the diplomatic telegrams he sent to the Quai d'Orsay. He would also use them later while writing his memoirs. In addition to their intrinsic interest, the diplomat's notes, which are necessarily objective, make it possible to counter the malicious insinuations of a few strong-minded people and biographers who are always ready to invoke the supposed 'mythomania' of Malraux.

Exactly as with his 1964 meeting in Peking with Mao, his 'off-the-cuff' conversation with Nehru was narrated, presented and reported by the writer in the third part of the *Antimémoires*, entitled, not without humour, *La tentation de l'Occident* (The Temptation of the West), and with great accuracy. Malraux first asks himself: 'What did I really know about this civilization?' Then he draws his host to one of his favourite areas: religions. As at their very first meeting, in Paris in 1936, Malraux asks Nehru 'a strange question', to which, no more than 20 years earlier, he had no 'satisfactory' answer to give: 'What enabled Hinduism to expel a well-organised Buddhism from India without serious conflict more than a thousand years ago? How did Hinduism manage to absorb, so to speak, a large and widespread popular religion without the usual religious wars?' But it was 1958, and since his first trip, a major development had taken place: India had won its independence from the British without a fight, even if it had to wage the terrible civil war of Partition with Pakistan in the process. Malraux, like Nehru, was interested in the modern country, in the formidable challenges it faced, and in its geopolitical situation vis-à-vis its gigantic and formidable neighbour, China.

After that, Malraux finally left to discover the south of India, of which he dreamed: Madras, Madurai, Bombay, Aurangabad; the sacred sites of Elephanta, then Ellora and Ajanta, which fascinated him, and had a profound effect on him. He would return to them several times, physically or in his books. Afterwards, he visited the new experimental city of Chandigarh, capital of the state of Punjab, built under the direction of his friend, the architect Le Corbusier.

Until Nehru's death on 27 May 1964, Malraux, who had in the meanwhile become Minister of State for Cultural Affairs, would meet him three times, in Paris: in 1960, during his official visit on the occasion of the 'Treasures of Indian Art' exhibition at the Petit Palais; in 1961, passing through Orly, where he stopped over especially for a meeting; and finally in September 1962, during a dinner at the Élysée Palace. A month later, China attacked India over border issues (still unresolved to this day), intruding on Indian territory before signing a ceasefire and withdrawing its troops in early 1963. One imagines that French diplomacy at the highest level must have worked to stop the conflict.

In 1965, Malraux embarks on a long journey to Asia, as far as Hong Kong, with a brief stopover in Bombay. It is at this moment, it seems, that the project of the *Antimémoires* was born in the writer's mind. Then, in August, he returns to India for his second official trip. In Delhi, he meets the new authorities, and celebrates the memory of his late friend, Pandit Nehru. He visits his cenotaph, then his house, which has become a national museum, a fact that is reflected in the *Antimémoires*. A tribute to the politician who wanted to 'create a fair State with fair means', an account of his testamentary wishes for the scattering of his ashes, and a meditation on death. The journey will continue as far as Benares, where Malraux—made honorary doctor of the city's Sanskrit University—gives a short speech of thanks, in which he takes up some of his favourite themes, such as the disappearance of Buddhism, and its 'absorption' by Hinduism. Finally, in the last of his official activities in relation to India, on 10 March 1967, he delivers a speech at UNESCO, in

Paris, for the inauguration of the 'Nehru and Modern India' exhibition.

In June 1969, after General de Gaulle left the presidency of the Republic following the calamitous referendum, André Malraux put an end to his ministerial functions, and would no longer accept any more from any others. This did not prevent him from expressing himself politically, from taking sides, and even from committing himself to the service of causes that he considered just.

Thus, in 1971, he rallied behind India led by Indira Gandhi, the daughter of Nehru, who, in turn, became Prime Minister, to come to the rescue of East Pakistan. This was originally Muslim-majority East Bengal, separated from its Hindu-majority Indian half in 1947 during Partition, and attached to Pakistan—a geopolitical aberration. Entering into a rebellion against the other half of Pakistan for its independence, the future Bangladesh would eventually obtain its freedom and become a sovereign state in the end of 1971, after India intervened and defeated the Pakistani army that came to invade the country and violently repress the Bengalis. Throughout this struggle, Malraux received diplomats, gave interviews, published appeals, and had even formed a mini International Brigade—at age 70—ready to go and support the cause of freedom with weapons in hand. Indira Gandhi gently dissuaded him from doing so. This episode, often misunderstood in France, gave rise to erroneous interpretations, even mockery. A few rare intellectuals, however, supported Malraux, including a certain Bernard-Henri Lévy.

In the spring of 1973, Malraux left for India, then Bangladesh. It was a private trip in theory, since the writer no longer held any official position, but his personality and his renewed support for India gave his stay all the appearances of a state visit. In Delhi, he was received by the authorities and met Indira Gandhi on several occasions. He then left for Agra, and subsequently Calcutta, before heading for Dhaka, the capital of Bangladesh, where he is received as a hero. He visits, inaugurates and gives speeches. Back in India, he goes on to visit Kathmandu, before ending his journey in Benares, and as on the last occasion, to Udaipur, Rajasthan. At the end of 1973, Malraux—after Martin Luther King and Mother Teresa, among other laureates—received the Nehru Award for International Understanding. It would be presented to him in Delhi at the end of the following year by Prime Minister Indira Gandhi, and it would be the pretext for his final trip to India. Delhi, then Udaipur, then Bombay—and his beloved Elephanta. Then on to Aurangabad, to see Ajanta and Ellora again, and finally back to Bombay. And goodbye to India. At least as far as the man Malraux is concerned. The writer, on the other hand, has long since integrated India into his cultural, historical and political universe, into his deepest reflexion, that on metaphysics, and into his work. Even if modestly. On the other hand, is it not highly symbolic that *L'Intemporel* (The Timeless), the third and last volume of *La Métamorphose des Dieux* (The Metamorphosis of the Gods) entirely reworked by Malraux until his last days, and published posthumously in 1976, ends with a superb evocation of the 'epic Civa of Ellora standing like a menhir'? This Nataraja who performs his Dance of Death 'on all that men have created', and invokes the pyres of the Ganges, and especially those of Benares, where it all ends. 'Towards night, the evening stars appear,' Malraux concludes, as if already on his way to an afterlife in which he would have liked to believe. And towards which new avatar?

VI

Gateway of India

In India's largest cities, such as in Delhi or Bombay, there is usually an India Gate. The one in Bombay is quite spectacular, facing the Arabian Sea and standing next to the venerable Taj Mahal Palace Hotel. It is a sort of great triumphal arch dating back to the colonial period, built by the British in honour of one of their sovereigns who came to visit the Raj, the flagship of the British Empire. Just like the English language,which has become Inglish, one of the bedrocks of the country. Quite a symbol! For we, western barbarians, do need at least one gateway, and a large one at that, if we are to have any hope of gaining access to a little bit of India.

In the Indian section of his *Antimémoires*, André Malraux writes,

> What did I really know about this civilization? Its arts, its thought, its history. Like that of the great

> dead civilisations—except that I had heard its music and that I had met a few gurus...I did not have the presumption of 'knowing' ... a thought that had resisted seventeen conquests and two millennia....

A fine and interesting passage, likely to elicit reflection, commentary, and to establish some, modest, parallelisms.

One will note this paradoxical mix of humility and boastfulness, which is not the least of Malraux's charms: he claims not to 'know' India, while mentioning his knowledge of its fundamentals. It is true that he said he had learnt Sanskrit on his own.... No one will quibble about his figures: no one thinks of counting the conquests that the country has undergone, ephemeral like the incursion of Alexander the Great, or long-lasting like the Empire of the Mughals, and who enriched its already fertile and diverse soil. As for the Indians, they are much 'older' than two millennia. According to specialists, India entered history with the first Indus civilization, around 2500 years before Jesus Christ.

Very interesting, on the other hand, is his sentence on music and gurus. Let us not forget Michaux and

'India sings'. Wouldn't music be the best door to open to try an approach to India? Especially when one is initiated by 'some gurus', in the broad sense of the term, synonymous with master, guide. So not necessarily men of religion, even if in India spirituality is everywhere and in everything, and if the sacred is never really absent from any form of artistic creation. Particularly music.

Before I even imagined going to India—my first trip was in the summer of 1981, when I was 24 years old—I had familiarised myself with its culture, including its music, in some rather surprising ways. And it was thanks to a few people who were my personal gurus. It all started with my taste for rock'n'roll, as a teenager. My favourite band was (and still is) the Beatles. Of the Beatles, whose separation was still fairly recent (1970), I had initially liked all the songs, signed Lennon & McCartney. Then, quite soon, as my ear became more sensitive, I learned to distinguish the differences in style between the two main songwriters of the group: John more rock, Paul more pop, in short. Later, I delighted in listening to the distinctive sound of the 'third Beatle', George Harrison. Not only a guitarist with a crystal-clear sound recognizable among thousands, but also the author of some of the band's finest gems.

Rare, barely one per album, and not all of them very well known, but always elegant and sounding more and more distinct. 'Love You To' (on the 1966 album *Revolver*, his first 'Indian style' song), 'Within You Without You' (on the 1967 album *Sgt Pepper's Lonely Hearts Club Band,* where he accompanies himself on the sitar, a formidably difficult instrument that he had studied in Bombay in 1965 with the master of masters, Ravi Shankar), 'While My Guitar Gently Weeps', 'Something...' Alongside the basic western instruments—guitars, bass, drums, piano—different sounds were introduced, difficult to define, but exotic: sitar, tabla, sarod, tanpura, enriching the Beatles' palette, and Indianizing it. Contributing to a kind of harmonious fusion, an aesthetic crossover. Harrison, who had 'converted' to Hinduism in the mid-1960s, had no choice but to feed his music on Mother India's udder! He managed not only to impose his songs and instrumentation on his band mates, but also, for a time, to interest them in India, in its spirituality and its artistic treasures.

George Harrison had been introduced to Hindu spirituality and had embraced it, before the hippies and their flower power, Kathmandu style, popularised it among all Western youth—in a form that is necessarily simplistic, even vulgar, and quickly appropriated by international business. Including music. Having become a disciple of Maharishi Mahesh Yogi, the inventor of Transcendental Meditation and one of those chic gurus for which India has the secret, Harrison had in turn influenced Paul McCartney, John Lennon and Ringo Starr, who were probably more tempted by the 'high' drugs and the nirvana they promised rather than by the real search for oneself or self-realisation. Except for Lennon, perhaps, who was the most troubled and the most receptive. Though his malaise, his personal quest for the absolute would find its outlet in political radicalism. In 1967, the guru had come to England on a high-profile promotional tour, buoyed by the fame of the Beatles. Mick Jagger himself fell under the spell.

In February 1968, George managed to get John, Paul and Ringo on board for India, with their small families, for a three-week meditation course at Maharishi's ashram in Rishikesh, in the state of Uttarakhand. This is a well-known resort, popular with the English for the freshness of its climate, on the banks of the Ganges and at the foot of the Himalayas. At the ashram, the Beatles were not on terra incognita: the cream of showbiz of the time met there—two of the Beach Boys, Donovan, Mia Farrow (then Mrs Sinatra)...

During this stay—of which the 'new' English journalist Lewis Lapham, the only lucky one who was allowed to enter the ashram and meet the stars, wrote a hilarious account, complete with photos[26]—John and Paul concentrated on composing, Ringo was bored. Only George went deeper into the practice of meditation. Subsequently, the other Beatles would move away from India, but not him. As a 'convert', he lived as a Hindu, composed as a solo artist, and after the group split up in 1969–1970, he composed a number of songs in which the Indian influence was noticeable: the well-known 'My Sweet Lord', for example, from 1970, a true paean to Hinduism.

But George Harrison was not content with expressing his 'Indianness' only through his music. As early as 1970, at the request of Ravi Shankar, he got involved alongside India in the drama of Bangladesh—like Malraux—by offering up his fame

26 Lewis Lapham, *With the Beatles* (Paris: La Table Ronde, 2007).

at the service of a just cause. And with the means at his disposal: there was no question of taking up arms, he organised The Concert for Bangladesh at Madison Square Garden in New York on 1 August 1971, thus unwittingly inventing what was to become the charity business, with its Live Aid, Band Aid and other such events with the resultant media and financial excesses that sometimes marred them.

'My friend came to me, sadness in his eyes', George sings on stage in his song 'Bangladesh', written for the occasion. The friend in question is obviously Ravi Shankar. Ravi Shankar opened the show by playing 17 minutes of his raga *Bangla Dhun* to a boisterous young audience who had come to see and cheer on some of their favourite pop stars: Harrison and Ringo Starr, but also Bob Dylan and Eric Clapton. Shankar, in a short speech full of modesty and humour—two of his cardinal virtues—had warned: 'Indian music is spiritual music. Please listen without making a noise or applauding'. And he had succeeded, by the grace of his own genius, in the service of the magic of India.

Harrison went on to write many more 'Indian' songs, to continue his study of the sitar and to return to India. When he died on 29 January 2001 in Los

Angeles, he asked that, after his cremation, his ashes be scattered in the River Ganges, in Benares, the city most sacred to the Hindus. Ravi Shankar, on his part, never left George, whom he considered his brother, noting that not only was he the godfather of Anoushka, his youngest daughter, but also his student. It is she who, after having accompanied the master on tour for several years, has now taken up the torch and the name, with the virtuosity, energy and respect that Indian music requires.

***

I had the great honour of being, towards the end of his life, friends with Ravi Shankar. We met in 2003. I had just published the French edition of *Bapi: The Love of My Life*,[27] Anoushka Shankar's intimate biographical book-album about her illustrious father, published in India in 2002. 'The writing was in the process of being completed when Harrison died', explains Anoushka in her dedication to 'Uncle George'. It was Pramod Kapoor, Anoushka's editor and Ravi's

27 *Bapi: The love of my life*, the first volume in the collection *Domaine indien*, which I was directing at the time at Cherche Midi 2. In the collection Family Pride, from Roli Books/Lustre Press.

old friend, who introduced us. One winter, in Delhi, at the headquarters of the beautiful Ravi Shankar Foundation that the master had created, which was both his home, the place where his archives are kept, as well as a place of residence dedicated to others, to musicians and his students, with recording studios, an auditorium for concerts, and guest rooms. The atmosphere is not like an ashram, although Ravi is loved and revered by all. The Shankar family lived there for about half the year, and come April, moved to their other home in San Diego, California. It was there that Ravi died on 11 December 2012.

But when I met him, he was wonderfully lively, simple, welcoming, and extremely funny. He was delighted to see his beloved daughter's book, a testimony of love and respect, filial as well as artistic, translated into French and published in France. Ravi loved France and Paris, where he often recalled that he had made his debut in 1930 on the stage of the Théâtre des Champs-Élysées as a graceful dancer in his uncle's troupe. This is why he had made it a habit, for many years now, to return to perform every May in this same Théâtre des Champs-Elysées. He recounted all this in French, and with much pleasure. I was quickly adopted by his wife Sukanya, an efficient and warm manager, and by Anoushka, who was shy at first, but with whom I got on well. I then saw the Shankars several times, either in Delhi, when I was there and they were there too, or in Paris, at every concert.

They were more than just concerts, they were ceremonies, but without any pretension, in the Indian manner. Before playing, while tuning his sitar with Anoushka's and the instruments of the other musicians, Ravi would explain his programme in a few sentences, the raga he was going to perform, many of which he had composed himself. He captivated the audience, preparing them gently. Ravi Shankar's music is the music of the soul, and this soul is the very soul of India.

The last time he came, he had agreed with infinite kindness to being interviewed in order to help promote his daughter's book. Music journalists rushed in, all dreaming of meeting the great Ravi Shankar. He was available, happy to be there, tired, of course (he was over 85), but still capable of a gourmet escapade in Saint-Germain-des-Prés to eat croissants at the Café de Flore! To thank them for their generosity, I had made Ravi and Anoushka wear two huge garlands of fresh flowers – marigolds, roses, jasmine, braided with palm leaves, similar to those that they hang at the entrance of houses in India, or are offered to the gods in their temples. The garlands had been made by a florist from Pondicherry in Little India, near La Chapelle, a neighbourhood I really like and where I sometimes go when Paris weighs down on me to recapture a little bit of my India. The dear man, to whom I had explained the whole story, had insisted, as an honour, on delivering the flowers in person, and presenting them to the Shankars. The scene in the lobby of the Prince of Wales Hotel was unreal. Everyone cried a lot, from joy, emotion and shared brotherhood.

After the concert, I went backstage to greet the artists. Ravi and Anoushka proudly wore their garlands. We hugged again, shed more tears. Then I took leave of my old friend, in the Indian way, like a son of his father, a disciple of his master: kneeling down and touching his toes with my hands. He, in turn, placing his hands on my head while pronouncing a blessing. That was the last time I saw Ravi. Too advanced in age, he then stopped touring. Listening to his music, I sometimes wonder if it was all just a dream.

Indian music, especially associated with dance in Bharatanatyam, has the gift of transporting the listener, even the barbarian, into another, transcendental universe. At the beginning, our ears are totally disoriented—in the strongest sense of the word. It no longer has any points of reference. Just as with Indian languages, in which we cannot distinguish any echo of our familiar Western tongues. And then we get used to it, we train ourselves to try to understand what we hear, what we see. Every movement of the raga, the slightest gesture of the dancer, has a religious significance that requires an explanation.

On my first trip to India, I was lucky enough to be introduced to Bharatanatyam by Roland Thomas, then director of the Alliance Française in Madras, and his wife, two afficionados who knew all the mysteries, all the refinements, and were willing to decipher some of them for me. Roland, especially, took me, one terrible monsoon evening, to see a performance by the divine Swarnamukhi, one of the greatest dancers of her time. Enchanting, dazzling, trancelike, thrilling. All the sensations that I had experienced at Ravi Shankar's concerts, which I also find in the processions in the streets or at the temples, at funerals—always with music, in India, as in southern Italy, melodies that are at the same time both funereal and lively. And even in the songs that blare in all the villages of Tamil Nadu, at the time of the temple festival, from the dreadful sputtering loudspeakers, perched almost everywhere. One would think they were Bollywood tunes? Not at all. These are episodes from the *Ramayana* set to music, whose heroes are named Ganesh, Murugan, Perumal or Shiva.

At the Monterey International Pop Festival in California on 16 June 1967, at the height of the hippie and counter-culture era, Ravi Shankar, who hated the excesses in which artists and the public indulged, and their irreverence, had demanded that the organisers, out of respect for the sanctity of his art, give him a separate time slot all to himself, during the day, rather than spending the evening sandwiched between two different performances. While recounting his 'feat' he said simply: 'I played for over two and a half hours sitting on stage under cloudy skies—a few drops of rain fell, but it passed—and I was inspired.'[28]

Ravi Shankar was, of all my Indian 'guiding lights', of my gurus, the most extraordinary, the most miraculous. He is India.

28 Reviewer Michael Church's account in the booklet of The Ravi Shankar Collection (EMI, 20)

VII

Gide and India

In the summer of 1946, André Gide, expressing deep weariness and, according to his daughter Catherine, 'an unusual anguish', confided to Jean Lambert, who was about to become his son-in-law: 'India, China... It is too late'.[29] These words can be interpreted as regret, given the age of the writer-nomad (almost 77), of no longer having the strength, or the desire to leave for the distant lands in question. Gide is not known to have shown any curiosity about China. With regard to India, the situation is quite different.

We remember what he had once declared to the Little Lady, a phrase that was noted and commented on later by Malraux: 'I am quite resistant to India; its dizzying quality has an opposite effect on me.' This 'dizziness', however, did not prevent Gide from

29 Jean Lambert, *Gide Familier* (Paris: Julliard, 1958).

taking a close interest in Rabindranath Tagore (1861–1941), the greatest writer of modern India and, to date, the only Indian Nobel Prize winner for literature. In 1913–1914, he published his translation of Tagore's *Gitanjali* under the title *L'Offrande lyrique* (The Lyrical Offering) with Éditions de la NRF. This collection of 103 poems, 'in praise of death', as he notes in his preface, was published in India in 1910 in its original language, Bengali, and then translated into English in 1912 and published in London. It is of course from the English that Gide worked—not without difficulty, he admits—on his version, which was announced as 'the only authorized one'. There seems to have been an editorial imbroglio concerning this work, for which the poet Saint-John Perse had apparently taken on the role of facilitator, introducing it to Gide. At the same time, in 1913, Tagore was awarded the Nobel Prize for his already considerable body of work. It is understandable that Gide wanted to have it exclusively in the catalogue of the NRF. As for what would have particularly motivated the translator in this text, 'is that it is not encumbered by any mythology'. The remark is rather unexpected, but can be explained by the fact that Gide, who had taken so many years to free himself from the one God of his Protestant youth, was hardly inclined to let himself be seduced by the 330 million or so deities of the Hindu pantheon![30]

His interest in Indian literature could have ended there. It did not. To begin with, the contact established with Tagore was maintained. In 1921, passing through Paris during a European lecture tour, the writer had lunch with Gide, who found him 'exquisite', a surprising adjective when one knows about the rather sensitive temperament of the Bengali Brahmin. But Gide, according to those close to him, had a very fine disposition, and he was able to get along with the most difficult people. And God knows if he did. Thereafter, the two writers continued to correspond. In a letter dated 27 April 1930, for example, Tagore thanks Gide for sending him *Strait is the Gate* (the English version of his *Porte étroite*), which made a strong impression on him and whose 'transparent simplicity' he praises.

A few years earlier, Gide had reaffirmed his taste for Tagore's work by translating another of his works, one of his plays, 'Post Office'. The text was published in 1922, under the title 'Amal and the King's Letter',

30 It is the Indian writer Vikas Swarup, the author of *Slumdog Millionaire*, who puts forward this figure.

a limited bibliophilic edition, illustrated with woodcuts by the Japanese Parisian Foujita, and never republished since.[31]

But karma made me discover another Indian translation by Gide, totally unknown and unpublished, in his archives where I was doing research for another Gidean project:[32] a thin grey-blue folder which bore, in capital letters, the title: *Translation of Kabîr Poems By R. TAGORE 22 Ff. Mss.*

These are 22 poems (one of which, III, is unfinished, plus a last unnumbered fragment), handwritten translations by Gide—and without, contrary to his habit, many repentances—of Kabir, an Indian mystic who was born around 1440 and died in 1518, translated into English by Rabindranath Tagore, once again, in a collection of one hundred texts entitled *Songs of Kabir,*[33] from which Gide worked.

Who is this Kabir, under whose invocation Michaux will place his *Barbarian in India?* How did it interest

31 Rabindranath Tagore, *Amal et la lettre du roi,* French translation by André Gide (Lucien Vogel, 1922).

32 *L'album André Gide ou la tentation nomade* (Paris: Flammarion, 2011).

33 *Songs of Kabir, mystical and emotional poetry,* translated by Rabindranath Tagore with the assistance of Evelyn Underhill (New York: Macmillan, 1915).

Gide enough to devote some of his time to Kabir in 1916? And what role does Tagore play in this story?

Kabir has been famous in India for five centuries, respected and indeed venerated by the Kabir-Panthis, 'those who follow the path of Kabir', one of the innumerable sects that irrigate the religious landscape of the subcontinent. Kabir still has several million disciples in India today, mainly in the state of Chattisgarh, in the centre of the country, in Benares (in the state of Uttar Pradesh, the land of the Brahmins) where he was perhaps born and spent most of his life, and in Maghar, near Gorakhpur, in the north of the same state, where he died.

His life is not well known to us, and it has been the subject of many legends, as well as of passionate debates among specialists. His date of birth is not certain, nor is one sure of the place where he was born. What is known, however, is that he was a *julâhâ,* a weaver, who spent most of his time in his little shop in old Benares.

His name means 'The Great'. In his poems, although he frequently speaks of his guru, Kabir never names him. What is certain is that he was deeply mystical, in the manner of the Sufis or yogis, but without belonging to any 'order'; that his intense fervour leads him to a single God, whom he designates by different names: often, simply, 'the Infinite'. And that his faith, which refers to both Islam and Hinduism, has a number of syncretic features. This explains why, shortly after his death, some texts attributed to Kabir were integrated into the *Adi-Granth,* the sacred book of the Sikh religion, which contains hymns composed by the founder, of Sikhism, Guru Nanak (1469–1539), as well as other spiritual gurus.[34]

As a result of his revelation, the humble weaver works less and less and preaches more and more about God and divine love. His shop becomes a place of gathering, of prayer and of teaching. This is not unusual in India, the most religious country in the world. But Kabir is not dogmatic in any way, and his words, free of all creeds, readily mock the bigots of all religions. At the same time as his reputation as a guru, or even as a saint, was born and spread among the people, Kabir's teachings were unsettling. At the

34 **Editor's note:** The Adi-Granth consists of verses by six Sikh gurus: Guru Nanak, Guru Angad, Guru Amar Das, Guru Ram Das, Guru Arjan, and Guru Tegh Bahadur. It also includes the teachings of spiritual leaders such as Ramananda, Kabir, Namdev and Sheikh Farid, among others.

beginning, he was taken for a madman, an enlightened man, but his heterodoxy soon got him into serious trouble. His enemies denounced him to the Muslim emperor Sikander, of the Afghan Lodi dynasty, who had him persecuted. He was even sentenced to death and had to flee Benares.

After that, Kabir would lead a wandering existence, preaching everywhere he went, and attracting a growing number of followers, even if not all of them understood what he was trying to convey. He died of old age, in 1518, not at his home in Benares, but intentionally in the village of Maghar, which had a sinister reputation: according to local legend, anyone who died there would be reincarnated as a donkey! This was the ultimate provocation of a free and facetious man, who demanded that he be allowed to die in solitude and meditation. Later, his disciples and even some princes fought over his body and his memory. A mausoleum was erected for him at Maghar, initially frequented by both Hindus and Muslims. But when clashes broke out, the Hindus erected a separate shrine alongside the first. Kabir was unfortunate in his failure to cure men of their intolerance and their folly.

As for his work, it is at least as conjectural and legendary as his life. Kabir did not write anything down. He was content to dispense, in a verbal and casual form, his teachings, through 'words', 'songs' or 'poems', to his listeners, some of whom later considered themselves his disciples. But all this was done in an apparently informal way, and without the weaver ever assuming the role of a guru, even if his fame, no doubt, did not displease him. This oral character remains in the texts attributed to him: 'a considerable mass, (...) several dozen books', estimates the Indologist Charlotte Vaudeville. The whole thing collected faithfully from his own lips, one hopes, and transcribed in the language of the region, North India, and of the time, in Avadhî, a dialect of old Hindi, mixed with Persian or Arabic terms. An apocryphal and composite body of work, whose most famous book is the *Bîjak* ('Seed' or 'Key'), a compilation attributed around 1600 to a man called Bhagvan Das and translated centuries later into other languages. It was from this considerable collection that editors, compilers and translators drew, each one making, according to him, the best selection: that is to say, keeping only what seemed authentic to him!

But what were the criteria? Here again, the opinions of specialists differ.

At the beginning of the last century, there was a translation from Hindi to Bengali of a large number of Kabir's poems by a certain Kshiti Mohan Sen. From these, Ajit Kumar Chakravarty selected 116, which he in turn translated into English. And it was this raw material that Rabindranath Tagore, assisted by Evelyn Underhill, then used. In his introduction to their collection, he explains the making of it. However, we do not know why the Anglo-Bengali duo only kept 100 poems from this preliminary work. No doubt to make a round figure, although Tagore's *Gitanjali* itself includes 103. It was from this book that Gide started in 1916, undertaking, in all likelihood, to translate it in its entirety, like the *Gitanjali*.

But why translate this Kabir, about whom he knew nothing? Perhaps simply to keep himself busy, not to 'lose his touch'. Because, in 1916, the writer, as his Diary attests, was going through a serious crisis: because of the war, of course; because of several of his projects 'running out of inspiration'; but also because of a return of religious preoccupations that were tormenting him. He even came close to converting to

Catholicism, before recovering, overcoming the ordeal and continuing his creative process.

Perhaps, in these troubled times in Gide's life, Kabir played a calming, anxiety-relieving role? We are reduced to conjecture, since only two mentions in the Diary, in February–March 1916, attest that he was working on his Kabîr, without any further details. We also do not know why he did not translate the hundred poems of the English collection (lassitude? technical difficulties?), nor do we know the reasons for his choice of texts, which was rather random: Gide translated poems I and II, left III unfinished, then moved on to IX, XI, etc., and did not go beyond XXXV. The ultimate sign of this lack of interest is that he would not publish his translations, which were put away in his files and where they have waited for nearly a century.

On the other hand, in 1922, Gallimard published a complete translation of the 'Songs of Kabir', which had in the meantime become 'Poems', modelled on Tagore's edition and translated by Henriette Mirabaud-Thorens. How did this project come about? Was Gide himself the repentant instigator? Their translations, without being absolutely similar, are very close. Another mystery. But in any case, given his eminent position in the house, he could not have been unaware of this publication. Especially since 1922 is also the year in which his translation of 'Amal and the King's Letter' was published. That is a lot of coincidences.

What is striking about Kabir is the liveliness of his language, his humour, his disrespect for institutions and taboos, combined with an exalted mysticism of great sensuality:

Rush to the feet of your Lover:
for your Lord stands by your bedside. (poem XIX)

The modernity of his approach too, which challenges religions in the name of Faith and makes the poet dream, in a country burdened for centuries by hatred between Hindus and Muslims, of communion and brotherhood at the feet of the same God, who addresses his disciple thus:

I do not live in Kailash any more than I live in Kaaba.
You will find me neither in ceremonies, nor in rites,
nor in yoga, nor in renunciation.

As Kabir, he who often 'speaks' at the end of his poems, says:

> *O Sadhu! The breath of all breaths is God.*

Gandhi had certainly read Kabir. And Gide, like many intellectuals of his time or those around him (Romain Rolland, Malraux, Pierre Herbart, among others), was impressed by the Mahatma's struggle and great persona. On 30 January 1948, he wrote in his diary these magnificent lines:

> Gandhi has just been shot by a Hindu. (...) Two days ago, a bomb had already been thrown at him. It was too beautiful, it was unhoped-for, this mystical victory, where spiritual fervour holds brutality at bay; my heart is swollen with admiration for this superhuman figure; swollen with sobs. It is like a defeat of God, a setback.

Gide could not have known Gandhi. On the other hand, he met Jawaharlal Nehru, the Mahatma's most distinguished companion and right-hand man, who was placed by him at the helm of India after

Independence. Nehru, as a young student in Paris, had visited Gide once. They had common friends. Then, thanks to a succession of coincidences, they crossed paths during the 1930s at La Pelouse in Bex, a posh Swiss boarding school for young girls from good families where Catherine Gide and Indira Nehru studied for a time as teenagers. A refuge for one, the illegitimate daughter of a married man who had managed to conceal his paternity and the existence of the child from his wife Madeleine, it is generally believed. As for the other, the daughter of a political fighter hunted down by the British and imprisoned several times for long periods; whose mother, Kamala, was treated in sanatoriums—first in Germany, then in Lausanne, where she died in February 1936, in her presence.

Catherine Gide remembered her friend as a young girl who was 'a little sad and very serious'. One would have thought so. In addition to the painful family circumstances she lived through, Indira was 'conditioned' very early on by her father, trained in political conflict, and even prepared to exercise power one day, who knows? We know the rest, and her extraordinary destiny. It is to be noted that Indira's surname, Gandhi, has no connection or link with that of the Mahatma. It was simply that of her husband, Feroze, but the coincidence proved to be a good one, and as a shrewd tactician, Indira used it well throughout her career.

Later, when Nehru came to power, we can assume that contact, however tenuous, was renewed with Gide. This is evidenced by two unpublished letters, dated January 1951, when the Indian Prime Minister was visiting France. On 19 January, Gide remembered his 'dear Nehru', whose career he had followed, and expressed his 'very warm friendship'; the next day, from his embassy, Nehru expressed his regret at not having had time, during his 'so short visit to Paris', to 'pay (his) respects' and assured him that, on his return to his country, he would think of him often. The exchange is somewhat formal, but warm, and Gide's English biographer, Alan Sheridan, affirms that the old man, on receiving the message, was delighted with it. Of a possible reunion, however, or an invitation to Delhi, there is no mention. 'It is too late'... Gide died a month later. He never went to India.

VIII

Connections

Apart from a connection with India, what were the associations between the writers who are brought together here by our imagination?

Our four barbarians belong to three different generations. Loti, born in 1850, is, in the eyes of the others, a man of the past. A post-romantic, who had chosen Chateaubriand as his master, someone from another time, born during the reign of Louis XV! When he created his NRF with a few friends of his own age, Gide set it up as a reaction against the literature of the previous generation, and more precisely, that of Loti.

In his journal, the author of *Aziyadé* features only twice, and that too, posthumously. In 1926, he refers to 'the Royal Society of Literature in London of which, eighteen months ago, (he) was appointed a member', specifying, with a nasty flippancy: 'replacing France (or Loti?)...'. Gide, who hated grandiloquence, the 'grand style', notes again, in 1932. 'Loti: in front of this Asianism, how much I feel Dorian!'

Born in 1869, a contemporary of Proust, Valéry, and Claudel, Gide, in addition to his own considerable body of work, wanted to act as a conduit, via the NRF and Gallimard, for the works of the writers he admired or discovered, whatever their nationality or era, but with a predilection for young talent. Among these were André Malraux, born in 1901, and Henri Michaux, born in 1899.

Gide and Malraux were friends. They knew each other for about 30 years. Malraux, who was the younger, was published in the NRF as early as 1928. In the 1930s, the two writers shared a common political commitment against all forms of fascism, which they actively fought. We see them at international congresses, side by side at the podium, or, in 1934, flying to Berlin, carrying a petition demanding the release of Dimitrov and the other imprisoned Bulgarian communists, falsely accused by the Nazis of the Reichstag fire. Hindenburg and Goebbels, to whom the letter was addressed, did not even receive them! After Gide's death, Malraux would remain faithful to him: he would preside over the society of his Friends, and would write a long preface to the *Cahiers de la Petite Dame* (Notebooks of the Little Lady), which is also an essay on the works of Gide and its posterity.

The author of only one real novel, *Les faux-monnayeurs* (The Counterfeiters), Gide is one of the writers most cited in *L'homme précaire et la littérature* (Precarious Man and Literature), the masterful treatise on which Malraux worked until his last days and which appeared, posthumously, in 1977. He also integrates Loti in his vast reflection, which closely resembles the problematic of his works on art. 'Loti's travels in Asia,' he writes, 'speak to us of people, of cities, more distant from us than the Orient of Lamartine or Chateaubriand'. No doubt, if we follow his thinking, because *L'Inde (sans les Anglais)* (India, without the English) or *Un pèlerin d'Angkor* (A Pilgrim of Angkor) are 'true-false' travelogues, while *L'itinéraire de Paris à Jérusalem* (The Itinerary from Paris to Jerusalem) is more 'authentic'. If you wish. But the journey of a writer is always transformed by his vision and his writing. And, in a way, the Khmer jungle of *La voie royale* (The Royal Way) is no more realistic than 'India of the palms'. It is true that it is a novel, even if largely inspired by Malraux's incredible expedition to Cambodia in 1923, with the discovery and looting of the ruins of the Banteay Srey temple. Literature knows how to transcend everything.

Michaux, who was also published at the NRF in 1927 with *Qui je fus* (Who I was), entered the Gidien circle in the 1930s. One of their letters, dated 1933, was found. In Gide's Diary, in 1937, his reading of *Ecuador* and *La nuit remue* (The Night Stirs) is mentioned with praise. The eclectic Gide very quickly showed himself sensitive to the universe of Michaux's 'early style', in which he undoubtedly found some echoes of his own humour, that of his 'farces' and of Paludes. But it was in 1941 that he embarked on an extremely rare adventure among writers, as an elder wishing to make known, or better known, a younger brother.

In the middle of the war, having taken refuge on the Côte d'Azur in the 'non-O' zone, the two meet by chance in Cabris, thanks to a mutual friend. However, as the precious Little Lady testifies, Gide has been 'rereading Michaux' for some months now, and 'he is definitely likes it a lot, to the point of being carried away'. Also, in these critical times when France is invaded and humiliated, the writer gladly accepts, as a diversion, Roger Stéphane's invitation to give a lecture in Nice, at the Hotel Ruhl, on 22 May 1941. The announced topic: 'Let's discover Henri Michaux'. Given the notoriety of the speaker, the room is absolutely packed. But, that very morning, Gide received a letter from the French Legion of Combatants, locally commanded by a certain Joseph Darnand, prohibiting the conference, on the pretext that the writer did not fit in with the 'spirit of sacrifice' that the Marshal intended to develop among the French youth! Gide, in fact, by virtue of his mores and his political positions, has always been one of the pet peeves of the zealots of the 'moral order', of the extreme right and, consequently, of the collaborators. As early as June 1940, in his journal, he had rejected Vichy, and rallied behind De Gaulle. After consulting with a few close friends (including Malraux), there was no further question of disengaging. Gide climbs onto the stage, and in a stormy atmosphere, makes a short statement in which he reads the letter from the Legion, and explains why, in order to avoid fights, he will not deliver his lecture. And, before leaving, he declares, not without panache: 'You have given me the greatest triumph of my career! Since it has not been read, the text of *Découvrons Henri Michaux* will be printed "hot" by Coueslant, in Cahors on 12 July 1941 on behalf of Librairie Gallimard, and published.'

The result is a slim booklet in which, in a personal and familiar tone, like that of the original conversation, Gide offers to read Michaux to his audience, explaining and quoting extensively from his favourite collections, *Ecuador* and *La nuit remue*. As a knowledgeable critic, he also talks about Michaux as a painter. Towards the end, modestly, he admits: 'Have we come full circle on Michaux? No, certainly not...' If for no other reason than that he does not have 'all his books at hand'. 'In particular, I miss *Un barbare en Asie*, which I regret not having been able to find in any bookshop or with any friend, and which I believe to be important above all else. Once again, with his customary generosity and extraordinary intuition, Gide had understood everything, and had succeeded in making people want to discover the universe of an author – unique among all.

What writer would not dream of such publicity? Gide's little book, only republished in 2001, had a considerable impact, even in other countries. Michaux, of course, expressed his gratitude to his prestigious patron. Though not without feeling some annoyance, it seems, as some letters to friends testify, at seeing himself thus 'reduced' to what Gide said about him. On the other hand, being pragmatic, he hastened to send Gaston Gallimard his next manuscript, *Au pays de la magie* (In the Land of Magic), in order to strike while the iron was hot. The publisher understood the message well, and the book was published at the end of 1941.

Malraux and Michaux were almost contemporaries, both of them having been honoured as young men by the gentlemen of the NRF, both attracted by Asia and having travelled there, they knew and appreciated each other. The friend of the latter, Micheline Phankim, testifies to this. But, if the worlds of their youth, that of *Royaume farfelu* and *Plume*, may seem to be in harmony, the careers of both men would soon diverge considerably. Malraux, a committed writer and successful novelist, opted for the limelight, even becoming a minister under General De Gaulle. While Michaux remained a poet, nothing but a poet, and a painter, shunning all publicity and fuss, and expressing nothing of his personal convictions. While the one sculpted his statue for eternity during his lifetime, the other did his utmost to erase all traces of his earthly passage. With the same pride, or almost.

Thus, in 1965, Michaux, to the great displeasure of Malraux, the Minister of Culture, refused the 'Grand Prix national des Lettres', a prestigious recognition of his work. And even, despite a number of requests, he persisted in his stance, declaring to one of his friends: 'Ah, that is indeed Malraux's idea! He wanted glory, he got it. Let him leave the others well alone! (...) Do you realise what would happen to me if I accepted? They would be forced to award me the Legion of Honour...'.[35]

Pure Michaux as he was, he refused to have his work included in the *Bibliothèque de La Pléiade* during his lifetime. Unlike Gide, Malraux and a few others... HM the loner and the rebel, the misanthrope, sometimes unjust, but consistent from his first texts, boiling with a dull rage. 'People like me must live as hermits, it's preferable', he wrote in *Un chiffon,* one of the poems from *La nuit remue* chosen and quoted by Gide. Michaux, a barbarian forever, removed from all the honours and glamour of the Republic? And, in

35 Testimony of Jacques Brosse quoted by Jean-Pierre Martin in his biography of Michaux, op. cit.

contrast, a Malraux who was fully integrated into the century? Without doubt.

In 2010, La Pléiade published Volume VI of the *Complete Works of André Malraux*, bringing together his essays. In the appendix to *L'homme précaire et la littérature* (Precarious Man and Literature), we find a number of fragments which are not integrated into the work; the writer, as was his wont, working in the form of folders, of more or less developed and accomplished thematic files. One, the first of Chapter VI, bears the following title, which perhaps, Malraux may have retained: 'To each culture its Barbarians'.

Postscript

Every time I find myself in India, every time I write about India, I feel, in Gide's beautiful words, 'inadequate'. It is inevitable, in the face of such vastness, such formidable complexity. On the subject of India, all the superlatives, all the hyperboles, all the reactions are not enough. They all fall far short of the mark. Not to mention generalisations, which are especially futile in this context.

Whoever would like to claim to know India, in its entirety and in depth, should first be born an Indian and a Hindu, without disregarding the minorities, both ethnic—in particular the hundreds of tribes, with their customs and dialects—and religions—Sikhs, Jains, Parsis, Muslims, Christians, Buddhists, Jews, and we are surely overlooking many others—that form part of the Indian identity. To master a civilization that spans 5,000 years. To speak, in addition to Sanskrit, Hindi and English, languages that hold the country together, the other Indian languages, in order to be able to understand the one billion three hundred million Indians who live in the sub-continent and to communicate directly with them. Particularly with these rural people, who, contrary to an image that the Western media complacently peddle—with the help of financial tycoons and Bollywood stars—remains 'the deep India', the majority and conservative base of the country. Regressive, some would argue. It would also take our Brahmin disciple of Pico della Mirandola to have visited every square inch of Mother India, as well as a few other Asian countries where Indian influence (primarily via Hinduism) has radiated: Sri Lanka, Nepal, Tibet, Cambodia....Without forgetting the countries where the diaspora is quite prominent: Reunion, Mauritius, Trinidad and Tobago, East Africa, Canada, the United States, Great Britain, France....The task, of course, is absolutely impossible, even if one had several lives. Eternity would not suffice.

So, faced with this infinite, everyone chooses for themselves their own India, builds it, or imagines it. Without any reservations. As Malraux reminded us, we are always someone's barbarian, anyway. Let us remember that etymologically, our 'barbarian' comes, via the Latin 'barbarus', from the ancient Greek word 'barbaros', a pejorative epithet formed with the help of an onomatopoeia, which designated, for the refined ears of the Greeks, all those foreigners who emitted formless sounds, an indistinct and savage 'brr-brr'. Since the dawn of time, the Other has been the object of suspicion, contempt and even hostility. Of curiosity, too. However, we prefer to go and visit them in their own country rather than have them come and settle in ours, especially with weapons in their hands! Just imagine the clash, not only military, but cultural, of the Huns against the Romans, the Arabs against the Franks, the Mughals against the Indians.

To approach India, even today, remains a gamble. Immediately, from the very first step on its soil, one must know if one is compatible—seduced, passionate, fascinated, in love—or otherwise. In either case, there is no need to insist. How many Westerners shun India for fear of poverty—why don't they look around! Or, worse, they go there and can't stand what they see. India is the mother of extremes.

After all these years, I still ask myself which is my India. The one of Loti, 'palms' in the south, 'famine' in the north, all impregnated with that mysticism which is inseparable from it, and which had also struck Michaux so much? Or the India that 'sings' that sacred music that had charmed Michaux and Malraux? Or this India, which has fought for its freedom and is still fighting to progress, but at its own pace and in its own way, nourished by its spiritual values, for which Malraux or Gide felt a deep empathy? All three, of course. About India, I love everything.

Even though I am not a Hindu, nor do I have several lives (after all, does one ever know?), I try to understand it as a whole. To complete, every time I read something about the country, or, better still, each time I return to it, my insane puzzle. For not a day goes by without Ganesh sending me a sign: be it the discovery of a new novel written by an Indian author; or an encounter with another passionate traveller; or, more simply, while reading French newspapers where, for better or for worse, India is increasingly present—even if not adequately 'treated' or explained as it should be. And not, as in the past, when the country was mentioned only when it was the victim of a calamity: a tsunami, a communal riot, an attack or a railway accident.

But my India, is it the 'real' one? Or am I not tempted by a form of idealisation? Maya, an illusion? As a traveller in love, of course, I am not unaware of the endemic problems of my adopted country: poverty, under-development, corruption, violence. However, it is not by erasing the colonial heritage for purely ideological or revanchist reasons that a country develops, but on the contrary by assimilating it, by re-appropriating it, by enhancing it. This is what the Indians, under the leadership of Nehru, succeeded in achieving perfectly in Pondicherry with the French heritage. It is true that the Pandit was a gentleman and a man of vast culture, open to the world, an atheist to boot, and not some demagogic politician. And that France had colonised only a small part of India, five modest fragments, which were bitterly disputed by the British. India, on the other hand, has succeeded in appropriating the English language, that Inglish which enchants travellers.

May the millions of gods of the Hindu pantheon ensure that low-brow stupidity never triumphs in India—but are we well placed these days to give it lessons in tolerance and democracy? And may my joy, born of an energy almost rising from the land, that penetrates me as soon as I return to Delhi, remain. 'I arrive in India, I open my eyes and I write a book.

Holy Michaux!'

Korkaddu, Juignettes, Paris, 2013–2014

Acknowledgements

I would like to express my gratitude, in no particular order, to all those who, in one capacity or another, have contributed to the existence of *Like Barbarians in India*, even without knowing it, a long time ago—and even from beyond. Sophie Hogg-Grandjean, Olivier Nora, Sophie de Closets, Sophie Charnavel, Dominique Fusco, Jérôme Laissus and the Fayard team. Micheline Phankim, Béatrice Foti, Catherine Gide, Jean Hugues, Tristan Savin, Hélène Amalric, Noëlle Meimaroglou, Valérie Dumeige, André Velter, Antoine Gallimard, Teresa Cremisi, Ravi Shankar, Elisabeth de Farcy, Philippe Héraclès, Marc Imperiali...

Some of the pages in this book have had a first life in a different form and context.